THE BENEFIT SYSTEM
IN THE
BRITISH THEATRE

by

St. Vincent Troubridge

The Society for Theatre Research

THE BENEFIT SYSTEM
IN THE
BRITISH THEATRE

THE BENEFIT SYSTEM
IN THE
BRITISH THEATRE

by
St. Vincent Troubridge

London
The Society for Theatre Research
1967

Printed by the Blackfriars Press Ltd.

Leicester

in 10 pt. on 12 pt. Georgian

CONTENTS

FOREWORD

This book about the benefit system in the British Theatre was left by the late St Vincent Troubridge, complete and ready for publication. It is the only full length study of the Benefit, and, as there may never be another, it is an irreplaceable exercise in research. The Society for Theatre Research is very happy to publish it, and deeply grateful to Pamela, Lady Troubridge, for her permission to do so. Originally the book contained 67,000 words, and cuts have been necessary. But, as these have been made almost entirely from a multiplicity of evidence and examples, it can justly be claimed that nothing of the argument has been lost.

The author did not supply a bibliography but a list of all books quoted in the notes has been printed on pages 160-163.

I am very grateful to Mr Basil Francis for undertaking the arduous task of making the indexes.

V. C. CLINTON-BADDELEY
General Editor of Publications
The Society for Theatre Research

PREFACE

Theatrical memoirs are not the most reliable of sources. Most were written in old age, with perhaps no more than a roll of playbills to supplement fading memory; some, as those of Lee Lewes, solaced the hours of imprisonment for debt; some, as with George Anne Bellamy, were "ghosted". There is also evident danger of distortion in the pious official "memoirs" of widows and sons — Charles Mathews, Munden and Charles Young. In many of these volumes, Tate Wilkinson for supreme example, the writer is at involuntary pains to display himself as mean, vain, vindictive and unreliable. Yet it is from these sources that we obtain our most intimate knowledge of the eighteenth and nineteenth century Theatre. It would seem to be a fair assumption that the evidential disadvantages of such works would not extend to those details of the benefit system and benefit custom which would be well known to all theatrical and many non-theatrical readers, apart perhaps from a mild danger, corrigible by reference to other sources, that the custom of the theatre might be strained a little to prove the memoirist right in one of his numerous and inevitable disputes.

With some reluctance, I have excluded benefits in fiction, as the material from memoirs and biographies is so abundant.

I am fortunate in having a number of authorities on theatre history as personal friends. Some of these have with courteous tolerance withstood the fire of my questions, or lent other help, and I should like to thank Miss St Clare Byrne for the loan of her copy of *The Road to the Stage,* Mr Laurence Irving for information on his grandfather, the late Malcolm Morley for the gift of a copy of the Rules of the Marylebone Theatre in 1837, Mr Richard Southern for enlightenment on the practice of 'laying the Pit into Boxes' at a benefit, Professor Arthur Colby Sprague for information and advice, and Miss Miriam Maisel for kindly verifying certain references for me.

I am also indebted to the Committee of the Garrick Club for permission to quote from John Rich's MS register of performances at Lincoln's Inn Fields Theatre and Covent Garden 1723-40, and from the Collection of Playbills in the possession of the Club.

St V. T.

INTRODUCTION

FOR ABOUT TWO HUNDRED YEARS, from the 1680's to the 1880's, the payment of actors and actresses was dominated by the system by which their weekly salary, almost always scanty except in the case of stars, was supplemented by the proceeds of the whole or a fraction of an annual, or more strictly seasonal benefit performance. These benefits were of various types, but all types had two common features—that the beneficiary was supposed to derive profit from them, and that he or she was the centre of attraction on the "night".

At one time authority frowned upon benefits, and in 1710 in his 'Regulations for ye Directors of ye Playhouse', the Lord Chamberlain ordered 'That no benefit plays be allowd, nor tickets given to any person'. But by then the benefit tide was already flowing too fast for this Canute gesture to stem it.[1]

It is now generally held that the benefit system was a blot upon a great profession, but, in fact, there is something to be said on both sides of the question, nor would the system have endured so long by sheer force of managerial imposition, had it not accorded with certain fundamental needs and desires of the players.

The disadvantages, as freely expressed during the entire period, and also as viewed from our modern standpoint, are very obvious. Of these the greatest was that it enabled the manager, more often than not himself in straits for money, to depress salaries by holding out the perhaps illusory inducement of the benefit, thus enforcing the actor to gamble unilaterally a possible half of his total annual earnings upon the incidence of popularity or the accident of weather.

The second main objection was more psychological than economic. It lay in the affront to personal and artistic dignity involved in the sycophancy necessary to secure a bumper benefit. The direct and degrading element of begging, in all but the highest ranks of the profession, included calling, hat in hand, with tickets and playbills, upon prospective supporters, and the need to avoid

[1] Allardyce Nicoll, *XVIIIth Century Drama 1700-1750*, Cambridge, 1925, App. B., p. 279.

giving offence all the year round to any single member, however offensive, of the limited play-going community. This latter obligation carried with it the unjust corollary that the tavern-haunting, intemperate, Thespian boon companion was likely to "make" a better benefit than the steady family man, who withdrew to house or lodgings between rehearsals to study his part for the morrow.

This second objection was put forward with force and dignity in the year 1800 by eight principal performers of Covent Garden, then in dispute with their management.

He must with unwearied industry canvass every friend and acquaintance, and urge their influence with their most remote connections. He must display, in large public companies whatever talent for conviviality nature may have bestowed on him; and this cannot be done but at a certain expence, and probably with a consequence worse than expence, the injury to his health.[2]

The last sentence is echoed with less dignity in a passage on an actor at Newcastle about 1812: 'as he opened an account at every grog shop in the town, his benefits were always fully, though not very fashionably attended; he used to call them "a meeting of creditors".'[3]

Tom Dibdin, actor and dramatist, writing in 1827, condemned the whole of this roundly as 'the pot-companion system . . . encouraged by the "nothing-loath" dashers of each town.' He adds a terrible comment by describing the four principal innkeepers of Harrogate in 1789 as gentlemen 'to whom no actor (if he wished to make a benefit) dare to speak with his hat on.'[4]

Another somewhat curious, though not enduring, objection to the benefit system was voiced in its early days by the first giant of the Restoration stage, Thomas Betterton, who complained to his successor Barton Booth of the difficulty of maintaining discipline with actors, as most of them, coming to the stage at the Restoration, were now middle-aged

and consequently more liable to fall into an inactive Negligence,

[2] *A Statement of the Differences subsisting between the Proprietors and Performers of the Theatre Royal Covent Garden, given in the Correspondence which has passed between them,* London, 1800, p. 39.

[3] Joe Cowell, *Thirty Years Passed Among the Players,* London and New York, 1844, p. 29.

[4] Thomas Dibdin, *Reminiscences.* London, 1827, I, 103-109.

or were only separately diligent, for themselves, in the sole Regard of their Benefit-Plays; which several of their Principals, knew at worst, would raise them Contributions that would more than tolerably subsist them, for the current Year.[5]

This was a particular complaint at a particular period, but there can be little doubt that an actor's performances of his stock parts would always be likely to suffer for two or three weeks in the bustlings, arrangements and anxieties prior to his "night".

Where then are the considerations to be placed on the other side of the account? There were two main advantages, one economic and the other psychological

The economic advantage arose from a good benefit representing the sole reasonable prospect of a player acquiring a lump sum, a little capital that could give him, if husbanded with discretion, just that vitally needed element of security against the chances of sickness or misfortune, though in all too many cases it had to go to the liquidation of debt contracted during the earlier part of the season.

Then, in an art depending for its expression upon the activities of the body and mind and the impact of the force of personality, it could not be other than natural for the artist to desire a position in which his financial success should depend upon an evening when, in a framework more or less of his own contriving at last — his benefit bill—, he should transcend the limitations of his usual "line of business", and for personal graces of body and skill of art, receive the personal reward of public adulation and golden guineas. There was the additional possibility of impressing upon the manager his aptness for better parts, and the ultimate Cinderella dream of the provincial player—that the 'unprovincial gentleman in a stage-box, who without applauding, lent an attentive and understanding ear to the doings on the stage,'[6] might prove to be an emissary from one of the Patent Theatres of the metropolis.

Another aspect of the benefit system was that it soon became a barometer of public favour. George Frederick Cooke, who came to Covent Garden in 1800 and achieved a startling initial success, so soon dissipated his position through continued drunkenness that by 1804 his benefit actually proved unremunerative, and in the follow-

---

[5] Colley Cibber, *Apology for the Life of Mr Colley Cibber, Comedian*, London, ed. 1756, I, 226.
[6] H. N. Hillebrand, *Edmund Kean*, New York, 1933, p. 96.

ing years he did not 'as it is termed, put his name up for a benefit.'[7]

The potential acquisition of a lump sum could also point the path away from the treacherous theatre for a disheartened player, though few were as frank as a young actor named Goodfellow, who took a benefit at Goodman's Fields in the 18th century, announcing that 'my friends having expressed a great dislike to my being on the stage, I have resolved upon taking this benefit to enable me to return to my former employment.' Actually Mr Goodfellow was not to be got rid of so easily, for when this benefit was well patronized, he remained on the stage in gratitude to the public.[8]

The benefit system had in practice a sufficient degree of the support of both parties, managers and players, to ensure its acceptance and continuance for two centuries. It died, not from any early type of strike or lock-out, but from a change in the method of presenting plays in London and the provinces, the "long run" system, in which there was no place for it.

---

[7] William Dunlap, *Memoirs of G. F. Cooke*, London and New York, 1813, I, 265.

[8] J. Doran, *Their Majesties' Servants*, London, I vol. ed., 1897, p. 348.

PART I
THE SYSTEM

I—ORIGINS

MOST APPROPRIATELY, THE FIRST MENTION of the theatrical benefit comes from that enthusiastic playgoer Samuel Pepys, under September 28, 1668.

Knipp's maid comes to me, to tell me that the women's day at the playhouse is to-day, and that therefore I must be there to encrease their profit. I did give the pretty maid Betty that comes to me, half-a-crown for coming, and had a kiss or two—*elle* being mighty *jolie.*

He did his duty, and reported 'the house, for the women's sake, mighty full.'[1] This was a collective benefit, and there is another indication of something of the sort in a theatrical contract of 1681, in which 'the days the young men and women play for their own profits only' are mentioned.[2]

Considered as a system, the origins are reasonably clear. It started as a special managerial concession to an exceptional leading lady, Mrs Barry, about the year 1686. Our first extensive knowledge of the practice and the etiquette that had already begun to surround it, comes with the documents in the Lord Chamberlain's records concerning the dispute between the players and the patentees in December 1694. It will be necessary to consider these documents further, but the rapid evolution of a personal concession into an established general right, and the equally rapid counter-moves of the quick-witted managers to transform an apparent loss of revenue into an instrument for keeping artists in economic subjection, are set out with admirable clarity by Colley Cibber,[3] who went on the stage in 1691.

The first Indulgence of this kind, was given to Mrs Barry . . . in King James's Time, in Consideration of the extraordinary Applause, that had followed her Performance: But there this Favour rested, to her alone, till after the Division of the only Company in 1695, at which Time the Patentees were soon

[1] Samuel Pepys, *Diary of Samuel Pepys,* ed. Lord Braybrook and Rev M. Bright, London, 6 vols., 1877, V, 366, 368.
[2] John Genest, *Some Account of the English Stage. From the Restoration in 1660 to 1830,* Bath, 10 vols., 1832, I, 369.
[3] Colley Cibber, *op. cit.,* I, 291, 292.

reduced to pay their Actors, half in good Words, and half in ready Money. In this precarious Condition, some particular Actors (however binding their agreements might be) were too poor, or too wise to go to Law with a Lawyer; and therefore rather chose to compound their Arrears, for their being admitted to the Chance of having them made up, by the profits of a Benefit-Play. This expedient had this Consequence; that the Patentees, tho' their daily Audiences might, and did sometimes, mend, still kept the short Subsistence of their Actors, at a stand, and grew more steady in their Resolution so to keep them, as they found them less apt to mutiny, while their Hopes of being clear'd off, by a Benefit, were depending. In a Year, or two, these Benefits grew so advantageous, that they became, at last, the chief Article in every Actor's Agreement.

The two earliest documents dealing with benefits, the 'Petition of the Players' and the 'Reply of the Patentees', both of December 1694, raise at the very outset of the system three matters around which endless dispute was to centre for two hundred years. The first was the frenzy of jealousy aroused in any actor's breast, should another, lower in the rigid heirarchy of the Stage—'my rank of salary' Tate Wilkinson was to call it later[4]—obtain any advantage considered to be undue through the medium of a benefit. Even the mighty Betterton was not exempt, for the Patentees make the point against Mrs Barry 'That Mr Betterton himselfe took notice y^t Mrs Barry made so great Advantage of a Play given her one day in ye Year that ye same wth her Sallary [which was 50/- a week] was more than his 5^ls p Weeke.'[5]

The second matter was that of "charges" and deductions from the gross takings of the benefit made by the management; the third, the alleged chicanery of the management in making sudden unilateral changes adverse to the player in the established customs of benefits—in this case the deduction of a third of the profits for the use of the Patent: subjects so important and involved that they must be considered at length presently.

---

[4] Tate Wilkinson, *Memoirs of His Own Life*, Dublin, 1791, I, 270.
[5] Allardyce Nicoll, *Restoration Drama 1660-1700*, 2nd ed., Cambridge, 1928, pp. 330-340.

II—THE TYPES AND TERMS OF BENEFITS

THE TYPES OF BENEFIT normally accorded to performers and theatre staff were five, the "clear" benefit, all charges of which were paid by the management; the "half-clear" benefit; the "benefit" proper, in which the performer paid an agreed, or at least a recognized, sum as "charges" for the use of the theatre and to defray the expenses of candles or other lighting, stage staff, orchestra, etc., receiving all profits above this sum; the "half" benefit, in which profits above the charges were shared equally between performer and manager, and the "joint" benefit, in which several lesser performers ("small people" was the disparaging term for them), were joined together as recipients of a whole or "half" benefit.

When a performer received a lump sum for the season or period of engagement instead of payment on a weekly or nightly basis, no benefit was due or taken,[1] except prior to 1750 when salaries were often expressed in a lump sum.

Plenty of other variants occurred in this land of compromise, and in 1703 Mrs Oldfield was stated to have agreed to a "two-thirds" benefit, though the lady contested this.[2] Betterton's famous farewell benefit in April 1709 was also, on the authority of No 1 of *The Tatler*, a "two-thirds" benefit after payment of "charges".[3]

Found at all periods, though perhaps most common in the 18th century, there was one other variant that might be called the "guaranteed" benefit. Mrs Barry, the original beneficiary in the theatre, made a second agreement with Betterton at a date between 1686 and 1694 by which, if the profits of her benefit, after payment of "charges", did not amount to £70, they would be made up to that amount by the patentees.[4] At Drury Lane in the season 1742-1743, Peg Woffington, whose salary was £7-10-0 a week, had a guaranteed benefit of £180, Mrs Pritchard had the same, and Mrs Clive, whose salary was £15-15-0 a week, had a £221 guaranteed benefit.[5]

[1] Richard Brinsley Peake, *Memoirs of the Colman Family*, London, 1841, I, 78.
[2] Allardyce Nicoll, *XVIIIth Century Drama 1700-1750*, p. 291.
[3] Robert W. Lowe, *Life of Thomas Betterton*, London, 1891, p. 180.
[4] Allardyce Nicoll, *Restoration Drama 1660-1700*, pp. 330-340.
[5] Janet Camden Lucey, *Lovely Peggy*, London, 1952, p. 80.

A later London instance indicates that this type of benefit could be an additional spur when a smaller theatre was resting its hopes for a successful season upon the introduction of a talented newcomer from the provinces. When George Colman the younger brought Charles Mayne Young to the Haymarket in 1807, the terms were

> We propose then, fourteen pounds per week and a benefit; you to take all the profits of that benefit ... after paying the established charges. Should there be a deficiency, we ensure that you shall clear one hundred pounds by it.[6]

The guaranteed benefit was an inducement also used by provincial managers towards stars reluctant to undertake long and uncomfortable journeys. At the Jacob's Well Theatre in Bristol in the 1740's, Mrs Pritchard, coming down to star from London, asked for and received a benefit guaranteed to £50 "clear".[7] Tate Wilkinson was applying the same pressure when in 1803 his offer to G. F. Cooke to visit York included "a *clear* benefit, ensured 60l."[8]

This type of benefit could be extremely favourable to a singer and a dancer. Mrs Billington had achieved an unprecedented success as a singer, and as such she was outside and indeed above the strict benefit rules applying to the members of the regular companies at the two Patent Theatres. Yet both theatres wanted her, and in 1802 her success was so great that she was able to drive the exceptional bargain of dividing her services equally between Drury Lane and Covent Garden. Each theatre, additionally to salary, paid her £500 in lieu of a benefit, and it may well be understood that it would appear unduly odd in those days for anyone to take a benefit at each of the two great houses in turn.[9] Thirty-four years later, when Alfred Bunn engaged Taglioni to dance, her terms were £100 a night for herself, two benefits guaranteed to produce her £1,000 and a half benefit guaranteed to produce her brother, who danced with her, £200.[10]

Stars other than singers and dancers could get extra concessions when they were in a strong bargaining position. Several such

---

[6] Julian C. Young, *Memoir of Charles Mayne Young*, London, 1871, I, 39.

[7] Sybil Rosenfeld, *Actors in Bristol 1741-8*, in *Times Literary Supplement*, August 29, 1936.

[8] William Dunlap, *op. cit.*, I, pp. 251, 252.

[9] James Boaden, *Life of Mrs Jordan*, London, 1831, I, 89.

[10] Alfred Bunn, *The Stage, both Before and Behind the Curtain*, London, 1840, II, p. 91.

relating to priority or choice of date are noted in Chapter IV, and for the season 1834-1835 the grasping William Farren, who was engaged for Drury Lane only, took advantage of the fact that his manager Alfred Bunn then controlled both Drury Lane and Covent Garden, and was able to stipulate for the performers of either theatre to play for his benefit.[11]

A "clear" benefit was the supreme desideratum. Not only did it result in a substantial increase in gain to the beneficiary, but it was the hall-mark of stardom. Its attainment was achieved by a nice equation between the importance and drawing power of the leading player, his or her business capacity, and the astuteness of the manager against whom that capacity was pitted.

Disputes about "clear" benefits are endemic in theatre history and memoirs. As early as 1694 'Mrs Bracegirdle demands one annual benefit the charges to be paid by the patentees'[12] to which the counter-offer was only one third of the profits of a benefit. The demand never changed, and in 1809 Mrs Jordan on tour showers abusive epithets upon Dimond, the Bath manager, who charged her £100, when she thought herself entitled to a "clear" benefit.[13]

A reduction in benefit status by the deprivation of the "clear" benefit could be used to discipline a recalcitrant or over-temperamental leading lady. With many others, Mrs Clive seceded from Drury Lane during the dispute of 1743, but in the subsequent settlement, she and Macklin were selected for "victimization", with a conspiracy between the two Patent Houses to re-engage them only upon identical reduced terms. Mrs Clive opted for Covent Garden, and as she put it in her justificatory pamphlet, *The Case of Mrs Clive submitted to the Publick,* issued in 1774, she

> yielded so far to the necessity of the time as to act under a much less salary than several other performers on that stage, and submitted to pay a sum of money for my benefit, notwithstanding I had had one clear of all expenses for nine years before—an advantage the first performers had been thought to merit for near thirty years, and had grown into a custom.[14]

Mrs Clive's figure of 'near thirty years' is of some interest, for it

[11] *Ibid.*, I, 55.
[12] Allardyce Nicoll, *Restoration Drama 1660-1700,* pp. 330-340.
[13] A. Aspinall, *Mrs Jordan and her Family,* London, 1951, p. 82.
[14] John Fyvie, *Comedy Queens of the Georgian Era,* London, 1906, p. 80. quoting *The Case of Mrs Clive submitted to the Publick* (1774).

indicates a time about ten years after the building of Covent Garden in 1732, and in ten years the rising element of competition between Drury Lane and Covent Garden may well have enabled the principal performers at either house to make their claim to a "clear" benefit as a custom if not a right.

The "half-clear" benefit, also referred to as a "clear-half" benefit, was, from about 1800 until the system began to decline in the 1860's and 1870's, at least as customary for a star or a leading man or leading lady as the normal benefit in which "charges" were paid, the "half-clear" benefit representing a rise in power by the managers, who were now able to resist the demand for a "clear" benefit in all but the most exceptional cases. In this type of benefit the beneficiary made an equal division of the gross receipts of the night with the manager, the latter paying the "charges". But the "half-clear" benefit is not without elements of possible confusion, for the expression was also used, though more rarely, for two other quite different kinds of financial arrangement, which will be detailed later.

Two instances from the career of Edmund Kean reflect the normality of the "half-clear" benefit. While still a provincial player, he obtained an engagement at the Olympic Theatre in 1813, from which he had great difficulty in extricating himself when a few months later his chance came to appear at Drury Lane. At the Olympic, though only to receive three guineas a week, he was to have 'an equal division of the house on the night of my benefit.'[15] In 1826, after twelve years of stardom, on his return from his second visit to the United States, he engaged Drury Lane, this time for twelve nights of performance at £50 per night, but again with half a clear benefit.[16]

On the slightly lower metropolitan levels, there were stars like James Anderson, who was certainly a great favourite in the "minors". With such actors the attainment of a "half-clear" benefit was a matter of luck and hard negotiating. In 1851, after his disastrous season at Drury Lane, Anderson played at the City of London Theatre in Norton Folgate, where his terms were £60 per week and "half a clear benefit."[17] But the next year, playing at the Maryle-

[15] George Raymond, *Life and Enterprises of Robert William Elliston*, London, 1857, p. 219.

[16] Alfred Bunn, *op. cit.*, I, 61, 62.

[17] James R. Anderson, *An Actor's Life*, Newcastle, 1902, p. 205.

bone for six nights, he could not do better than sharing terms of a clear third of the receipts and half a benefit—not, it should be noted, half a "clear" benefit.[18]

In the provinces we also meet the "half-clear" or "clear-half" benefit at different dates. Joe Cowell's terms when on the York circuit in 1816 as a comedian, were 'to visit seven towns in a year . . . and have half the clear receipts of one night in each for a benefit.'[19] John Coleman, playing in East Anglia about 1851, was offered 'another benefit (this time a clear half of the receipts).'[20] The "clear-half" benefit was mentioned in those words by George Vandenhoff[21] on the subject of his engagement at Liverpool in 1840, and he adds that his benefit was about £90. The Liverpool Theatre held £300 then, but times were bad in 1840, and it looks as if the house was £180, the manager paying the "charges".

One of the unusual arrangements liable to cause confusion was when for some reason or another, the usual "charge" for the night to the beneficiary was halved. The word "half" would then be applicable to the "charges", and though it was not strictly a "half-clear" benefit, it may have been referred to thus, as a contraction for "half clear of charges." It was certainly not a "half" benefit, for the beneficiary received the total receipts, less a halved "charge" and not half the receipts less a halved "charge". It was a benefit of this nature that Macready took at Birmingham in 1826, for we are told the "charge" (£26-10), which was about half the normal for that time and place.[22]

But there was yet a third type of arrangement, prevailing more in the 18th century, to which the term "half-clear" benefit could be applied. This was when a star received two benefits in a season, one "clear" and the other subject to normal "charges". Garrick had such a contract in his first season at Drury Lane in 1742,[23] and so had Mrs Billington at Covent Garden in 1786.[24]

"Clear" benefits could be divided into still smaller fractions, and James Anderson, playing a short season with Webster at the Haymarket in 1845, received £100 for twelve nights, and a clear third of

[18] *Ibid.*, p. 208.
[19] Joe Cowell, *op. cit.*, p. 33.
[20] John Coleman, *Fifty Years of an Actor's Life*, London, 1904, II, 554.
[21] George Vandenhoff, *Green Room and Stage*, London, 1860, p. 107.
[22] W. C. Macready, *Reminiscences*, ed. Pollock, London, 1875, I, 310.
[23] Percy Fitzgerald, *Life of Mrs Clive*, London, 1888, p. 31, note.
[24] *Memoirs of Mrs Billington*, London, 1792, p. 37.

a benefit.[25] These were not good terms, but Anderson was still making his way as a leading man in 1845.

The benefit proper and the "half" benefit call for no especial comment, but there are some points of interest in the joint benefits of the "small people". Where two only shared a benefit this was known as a "double" benefit.[26] Careful calculation of figures must often have been necessary, as when in 1709 Mrs Willis and her daughter Mary were engaged at Drury Lane at annual salaries of £40 and £20—that of the leading lady Mrs Oldfield was £200—and "to have a share in a benefit play in proportion to their salaries."[27] On the other hand there were rougher and readier methods, especially in the country, of determining the benefit shares of "small people". Thomas Snagg, who strolled in the mid-18th century, and once played with Garrick, says 'These [benefits] of the same rate [of salary] were determined by the dice', adding cynically, 'sometimes per favour, especially a pretty female may have secret interest with the Manager.'[28] It is a Hogarthian picture to visualise Osric, Rosencrantz, the Second Gravedigger and Guildenstern dicing on the drum to determine which should share a benefit.

The theatre staff who were included in the system were the Manager, whether or not he also played, the Treasurer, the Box-book-Keeper, the Prompter, and the leader of the Band. These four officials of the theatre received benefits with regularity virtually throughout the two hundred year period. The box-keepers are noted as taking a benefit at Drury Lane as early as 1705.[29] At the Theatre Royal, Dublin, in 1825, Mr Lowther, the box-keeper, 'announced his farewell benefit, accompanied by a statement that he found the emoluments of his situation insufficient for the increasing claims of his family, and that he had resolved to retire from the post.'[30]

The position of the Manager, most important of the four officials, was the least constant, and demands some examination.

When a manager who also played took a benefit, the question arose of his two capacities and the distinction between his personal emoluments and the managerial coffers in which partners might be

[25] James R. Anderson, *op. cit.*, p. 132.

[26] Charles Lee Lewes *Memoirs*, London, 1805, I, 29-31.

[27] Allardyce Nicoll, *Restoration Drama 1660-1700*, pp. 330-340.

[28] Thomas Snagg, *Recollections of Occurrences*, London, 1951, Note 7.

[29] Charles B. Hogan, *Shakespeare in the Theatre, 1701-1800 (London 1701-1750)*, London, 1952, p. 4.

[30] *History of the Theatre Royal, Dublin*, Dublin, 1870, p. 62.

concerned. Tate Wilkinson, who was frequently delighted at the rectitude of his own conduct, speaking of his benefit at Sheffield in 1784, says 'Observe, kind reader, that at those benefits at Sheffield, or any where, I never take more than half.'[31]

From Garrick's retirement in 1776 onwards, a race of managers who were not actors arose, such as the Harrises, Sheridan and the two Colmans, and the custom of the managerial benefit fell into desuetude, except where the manager also acted, as did John Kemble at Covent Garden from 1803. It lingered for another eighty years in the provinces.*

The remaining officials of the theatre who might expect to receive benefits individual or collective, fall into the two categories of the permanent "front of house" staff, as it is now called, the "numberers", to use an Elizabethan word of long survival, and their like, as one category, the other containing those auxiliaries whose importance and even presence varied with different theatres and different periods.

Of the permanent staff, early benefits have been noted at Drury Lane and Lincoln's Inn Fields for the "pit office-keeper" (1715), the "gallery, box-and-door-keepers" (1715), the "numberer and gallery box-keeper" (1731), the "supervisor and sub-treasurer" (1736)[32] and the "pit-door-keeper" and three others (1762).[33] In the more genial atmosphere of the provinces, when a popular door-keeper at Perth was given a benefit in 1837 after many years of service, the organizers of the affair insisted that he should play a small part in a play that night.[34] But in the main after Garrick's day, these lesser front of house officials received their equivalent remuneration through "ticket nights", which are described later in this chapter.

The names of certain other officials may be found as beneficiaries in isolated cases. In the first half of the 18th century we find the dancing-master (1724), the ballet-master (1749), and somewhat astonishingly the petit-maître (1730), though his theatrical function remains undefined.[35]

---

* It is impossible to fix an absolute date. The manager of the Theatre Royal, Exeter, always took a benefit during the pantomime season and was still doing so as late as 1928, when it was advertised in the local paper. V.C.C-B.

[31] Tate Wilkinson, *The Wandering Patentee*, York, 1795, II, 160.
[32] Charles B. Hogan, *op. cit.*, pp. 11, 37, 48.
[33] Percy Fitzgerald, *Life of David Garrick*, London, 1868, II, 479.
[34] Peter Baxter, *The Drama in Perth*, Perth, 1907, p. 242.
[35] Charles B. Hogan, *op. cit.*, pp. 27, 36, 81.

Sometimes at minor theatres in the 19th century, the house-author would get a weekly salary and two benefits per season instead of the usual author's nights.[36]

In the early 19th century the costumier to a theatre usually received a benefit (though not at the Patent Theatres), as did also the tailor and wardrobe-keeper to the theatre at Bath in 1844—but only after sixty-four years service.[37] Presumably the costumier also enjoyed an additional nice little perquisite of hiring dominos when in 1849 at Norwich, the opera of *Gustavus the Third* was produced for his benefit, and the management admitted the box patrons on the stage to the Masked Ball incidental to the piece.[38]

There is a pleasant echo from Nell Gwynn in the benefit granted at Hereford in 1788 to the fruiterer to the theatre and his wife. More dubious is the benefit in the same Hereford season "for the builder", as this appears to be a device by the manager to shuffle off onto the public his obligations to the carpenter who had fitted up stage and auditorium.[39] Last noted of these occasional staff beneficiaries is the Master of the Ceremonies at Brighton in 1829, who was a Lieutenant-Colonel and netted £80 by a benefit of an Italian opera.[40]

There remains the stage-manager, who always acted in addition to his other duties, and took his benefit as a player, though with an element of added priority of date. An exception is the case of Wroughton, stage-manager of Drury Lane at various times from 1796 to 1814, for he 'received £100 for a benefit, merged in my weekly salary.'[41] Another example of the flexibility of which a stage-manager's appointment allowed is given in a letter containing an offer of the stage-managership at Sadler's Wells in 1826, which concludes, 'Feeling this offer is one pound per week less than that mentioned in our former treaty, I would willingly make it up by . . . throwing you off an equivalent in the scale of your benefit charges.'[42]

One other still lesser form of theatrical benefit can be distinguished. This was when an artist had performed services which

---

[36] Thomas Dibdin, *op. cit.*, I, 434, 438. Dibdin, when house-author at the Surrey about 1812, received £15 a week and two benefits, paying £70 "charges".

[37] S. Penley, *The Bath Stage*, London, 1892, p. 144.

[38] Bosworth Harcourt, *The Theatre Royal, Norwich*, Norwich, 1903, p. 57.

[39] Cecil Price, *The English Theatre in Wales*, Cardiff, 1948, p. 79.

[40] H. C. Porter, *History of the Theatres of Brighton from 1774 to 1886*, Brighton, 1886, p. 59.

[41] Thomas Dibdin, *op. cit.*, II, p. 81.

[42] *Ibid.*, II, pp. 323, 324.

demanded an acknowledgement but hardly qualified for a benefit. The management then granted the artist a number of "tickets", presumably for an evening when it was not anticipated that the house would be full, to be sold for his or her own benefit. Mrs George Anne Bellamy when on the down grade in 1786, had recourse to this device.

> At the conclusion of the season I made application to Mr Younger, acting manager of Drury Lane, to request that the proprietors would grant me a number of tickets; as I could by no means expect the same indulgence either from patentees or performers, I had experienced the year before at Covent Garden [i.e. a benefit]. They were immediately granted; and the late Earl Spencer requesting his lady to honour me with her patronage, in addition to my former patronesses, I met the success I hoped for.[43]

This form of benefit is mentioned later by Mrs Becky Wells of her early days at York about 1773.

> But from the respectability of our introductions, the manager engaged me for three nights, and allowed me on the third to send in tickets, which turned out much to our advantage, as we were on friendly terms with some of the first families, from whom we received many marks of kindness and regard.[44]

In the case of Mrs Bellamy, this practice, no doubt, verged upon the charitable, but it is of interest that, in both cases, even for a ticket night, the elaborate machinery of patronage had to be invoked. When Garrick in 1750 desired to help Farquhar's daughter, who was still alive, this also took the form of admitting her tickets upon a certain night.[45] The ticket night could be a form of vicarious pension. At Bath an old actress, Miss Summers, who retired in 1820 after fifty years' service with the company, was allowed a ticket night each season for life.[46]

One still more complicated arrangement is found in the 18th century, for when Everard played at Jacob's Well, Bristol, in 1765, his benefit terms were 'to be allowed to sell five pounds worth of tickets by way of benefit; and if I should bring in more, half was to

---

[43] *Life of George Anne Bellamy*, London, ed. 1785, V, 87.
[44] *Life of Mrs Sumbel, late Wells*, written by Herself, London, 1811, I, 27, 28.
[45] Percy Fitzgerald, *Life of David Garrick*, London, 1868, II, 473, 474.
[46] S. Penley, *op. cit.*, p. 119.

go to the managers.'[47] This seems in fact to have been a combination of the "guaranteed benefit" with the "ticket night."

By the early 19th century the granting of tickets had crystallized into "Ticket Nights", of the operation of which there is a clear though critical account in a Liverpool theatrical newspaper of 1821.[48]

> Last evening was what is called a Ticket Night, three or four of which occur during the Benefits. Each of these Ticket Nights is made up of from four to eight, (at the Manager's option) of the door-keepers and servants about the theatre, who are allowed, on these occasions, to sell as many tickets as they can, the amount of which is divided between the Managers and these individuals; thus, we will suppose one of the door-keepers disposes of tickets to the amount of twenty pounds, for this privilege he must pay the Managers ten pounds; the remaining ten pounds are for himself, out of which, however, he has the expences of printing to pay (the managers will not pay a farthing), and to suffer the loss incident on the distribution and collection of a number of Tickets—*All the money* which happens on those nights, to be paid at the doors is pocketed by the Managers.

That was the procedure at Liverpool, though it is to be doubted whether the beneficiaries of "ticket nights" always had to pay the expenses of the printing of the tickets, but elsewhere it seems that minor artists could also take ticket nights, as less hazardous than benefits, and so could individual heads of departments backstage, for instance the master carpenter at Brighton, as early as 1791.[49]

At Dublin by the 1840's these ticket nights had been consolidated, and at the end of the season, a "half" benefit was shared by "the leader of the chorus, the ushers in front and the ticket takers',[50] the house being always a "bumper."

A benefit could also be granted as a form of additional reward or encouragement. This had been, indeed, the inception of the system with Mrs Barry in 1686, and cases may be noted in the most varied circumstances throughout the two centuries of its duration. Lavinia

[47] E. C. Everard, *Memoirs of an Unfortunate Son of Thespis*, Edinburgh, 1818, p. 7.
[48] *Liverpool Theatrical Investigator*, Liverpool, 1821, I, 515.
[49] H. C. Porter, *op. cit.*, p. 17.
[50] Lester Wallack, *Memoirs of Fifty Years*, London, 1889, p. 49.

Fenton, the original exponent of Polly Peachum, was given two benefits at Lincoln's Inn Fields in the first season of *The Beggar's Opera* in 1728 (surprisingly the second was not a very good one),[51] as was Mrs Jordan in her first season at Drury Lane in 1786.[52] Henry Woodward, who played Harlequin as well as light comedy gallants at Drury Lane during Garrick's reign, received an extra benefit each season for doing so.[53] But a reward of this kind was likely to develop into a supposed right, and it was the refusal by Quin of a second benefit that caused Peg Woffington's departure in 1751 from Covent Garden to Dublin, where she received from Thomas Sheridan £400 a year and two clear benefits.[54]

The graver theatre lovers at the turn of the 18th and 19th centuries disapproved of the introduction of the second benefit during the season as a reward for notable success. Mrs Jordan's biographer writes, 'The managers had tripled her original salary, and given her two benefits in the season; an innovation first made for Mrs Siddons, and very idly made.'[55]

This was not literally true, for, as has been seen, Lavinia Fenton had been granted two benefits as far back as 1728, but it was certainly a revived custom. Besides the inevitable jealousy aroused, the second benefit had the disadvantage (to be discussed more fully later) of forcing stars into quite unsuitable parts in their desperate search for benefit attractions.

When John Henderson was brought out by Colman the elder at the Haymarket in 1777 as an aspirant for the star position rendered vacant by Garrick's retirement the year before, the engagement had been for a lump sum for the season without a benefit, but the newcomer's success was so great that the manager not only granted him a benefit, but, as an additional pleasant surprise, did not inform him till next day that the benefit had been a "clear" one.[56] Unexampled success also caused G. F. Cooke's benefits to be given him "clear" on both his first two seasons at Covent Garden in 1800 and 1801.[57] Garrick, whose arrangements were frequently flexible, even used the benefit as what would now be called an introducer's commission. An

[51] John Rich's MS. Register of performances at Lincoln's Inn Fields Theatre, 1723-1740, in possession of the Garrick Club.

[52] John Fyvie, *op. cit.*, p.363.

[53] Percy Fitzgerald, *Life of David Garrick*, I, 327, 328.

[54] John Fyvie, *op. cit.*, p. 363, and Janet Camden Lucey, *op. cit.*, p. 164.

[55] James Boaden, *Life of Mrs Jordan*, I, 84, 85.

[56] R. B. Peake, *op. cit.*, II, 7, 8.

[57] William Dunlap, *op. cit.*, I, 166.

actor, Thomas Sheridan, the dramatist's father, then playing at Drury Lane, brought the manager a comedy by his wife: on acceptance he was allowed to play the principal part himself, and, as the play proved very successful, he was donated a benefit for his services.[58]

When the manager was of high standing the nature of the benefit to be taken could be left indeterminate. Mrs Yates wrote to Garrick in 1774 about her terms of engagement, 'as to a Benefit, you shall settle that yourself.'[59] In 1842 'Mrs Nisbett and her mother called' on Macready to discuss an engagement, and 'She waived the question of a Benefit, leaving it to circumstances and my consideration.'[60]

There remain a few more isolated examples of exceptional types of benefit to be considered.

As the cost of living and consequently the overheads of theatrical production started another climb after the end of the Napoleonic Wars, it became unreasonable that an artist obtaining the very highest nightly salary for an often brief engagement should also expect to take from the managerial treasury the proceeds of still another night as a benefit. The tight-fisted Taglionis of the theatre, if their attraction was truly exceptional, still obtained their own terms, but, in general with the stars who received the top nightly figures for their services, there crept in a new phenomenon that might be called the "nominal" benefit: it was the first portent of the decline of the whole system. By the 1830's the word benefit still held most of its ancient magic and could be relied upon to fill the house, so the virtue of the charm must not be wasted, whether the performer or the management reaped the profit. The nature of the "nominal" benefit is well illustrated by the following extract from the contract between Alfred Bunn and Madame Malibran of 1835 (which is here translated from the French original).

> Madame G Malibran shall lend her name for a benefit night on the twentieth performance, the receipts of which in their entirety shall belong to the management, Madame Malibran renouncing in advance any payment for this twentieth performance.[61]

[58] Thomas Davies, *Memoirs of the Life of David Garrick*, London, 1780, I, 302.

[59] *The Private Correspondence of David Garrick*, ed. Boaden, London, 1831, I, 623.

[60] *Macready's Diaries*, ed. Toynbee, London, 1912, II, 161.

[61] Alfred Bunn, *op. cit.*, I, 241.

There has always been quite friendly and unmalicious mockery of the prolonged "farewells" of stage folk reluctant to quit the scene of their histrionic triumphs. On the benefit side, or within the benefit system, there was, on the whole, during the 18th and early 19th centuries less of this lingering than in the later days of repeated farewell tours of the provinces. There was an enormous all-star "farewell" benefit, often at Drury Lane after about 1860, and then the curtains closed on retirement. But the term "farewell" began to be abused slightly from the end of the 1820's, when stars acquired the habit of going off for a year or more to acquire their pile of dollars in a visit to the United States, and did not see why they should not also take a temporary farewell of their English admirers. Charles Kean took a "farewell' benefit at the Haymarket in June 1839 that seems rather forced on the face of it as it followed a season of only twenty-two performances. Though he did in fact go to America two months later, this does not seem to have been a sufficient reason for the use of the word.[62] But there are other instances in which the impending visit to America was definitely the occasion of the "farewell", and one such was Madame Vestris's benefit at Covent Garden in 1838, shortly after her somewhat over-due marriage to Charles Mathews the younger (intended to mollify the moral susceptibilities of the Yankees), when she played the leading parts in both an opera and a comedy and cleared nearly a thousand pounds.[63] E. A. Sothern, creator of the famous character of the whiskered "swell" of the 1860's, Lord Dundreary, always behaved handsomely, and set a higher standard when he handed the proceeds of his pre-American farewell benefit at the Haymarket in 1871 to the Royal General Theatrical Fund.[64]

It is interesting to notice how in a period of not much over half a century theatrical conception and custom on some aspect of the benefit system could come right round to the exact opposite of its beginnings. In 1781 anything in the nature of a prolonged run for a piece was a great rarity, and continuity of performance must not be broken if possible, especially at the Haymarket with its limited season confined to the summer months only. So, when George Colman found himself in possession of a solid success with

[62] John Cole, *Life and Times of Charles Kean*, London, 1859, I, 302.

[63] Malcolm Mackintosh (The Old Stager), *Stage Reminiscences*, Glasgow, 1866, p. 84.

[64] T. Edgar Pemberton, *Memoir of E. A. Sothern*, London, 4th ed., 1890, p. 108.

O'Keeffe's *The Agreable Surprise* in that year, he took the necessary steps. 'Most of the nights to come of the Haymarket short season were fixed for the performers' benefits; but Mr Colman purchased many of them from the performers, that *The Agreable Surprise* might not be stopped.' [65]

Yet by 1855, when the modern long-run system was beginning to gather headway, Mr and Mrs Charles Kean, who had a very success-ful revival of *Henry VIII* running at the Princess's, took a different view and broke this run for their benefit, 'when a change of per-formance was substituted as a compliment to their immediate patrons and friends.' [66]

Though sixteen years later in time, what is really an intermediate position with the old and new conceptions still at odds, is revealed by the terms of the engagement of James Anderson at Drury Lane in 1871 to play Anthony in *Anthony and Cleopatra*. Though the play was put on for a run, Anderson's terms still included "half a clear benefit", and the older rules of the beneficiary's selection of a benefit play, regardless of breaking a run, still seem to have applied. Ander-son put up *Macbeth* for his benefit, and the leading lady, Miss Wallis, put up *Romeo and Juliet* for hers. [67]

[65] *Recollections of the Life of John O'Keeffe, written by Himself*, London, 1826, II, p.7.

[66] John Cole, *op. cit.*, II, 140.

[67] James R. Anderson, *op. cit.*, p.315.

III—THE BESPEAK

THE BESPEAK, WHICH FLOURISHED MOSTLY in the provinces, was somewhat different to a benefit, although beneficiaries sometimes applied the word incorrectly to the patronage they received at their benefits. In fact the bespeak, in which some local magnate or body "bespoke" a play, selected it, and either bought for distribution a large number of tickets or paid a subsidy of a certain number of guineas, was always a managerial or company affair, in which it differed from patronage at an individual benefit. It was connected in the 18th century with the necessity to obtain the licence of the local magistrate for performance; once he had been convinced by the manager that the entertainments were not undesirable, it was a natural step for him to bespeak a play; or, if the licensing magistrate were not theatre-minded, his approval and his name could be used in approaching other influential personages in the neighbourhood.

The distinction between a benefit and a bespeak is brought out by an episode in which no less a person than David Garrick confused the two. In 1758 Tate Wilkinson was playing at Portsmouth, and at that time Garrick regarded him as a clever young actor whom he proposed to engage for Drury Lane next season. Mr and Mrs Garrick were staying with Dr and Mrs Gerney nearby, and Wilkinson's benefit coming round, Garrick, wishing to do his protegé a kindness and not being very conversant with the theatrical terms and customs of the provinces where he never played, 'fixed a bespeak' together with his holiday host, saying 'We desire, Wilkinson, you will fix on a favourite character.' But the intended kindness proved double-edged, for though the name and presence of the great actor no doubt filled the house, the company maintained that as the occasion was a bespeak, this made it a company celebration and deprived Wilkinson of his normal beneficiary's right to select the pieces in the bill. It is to be supposed that such a conflict would be referred to the Portsmouth manager for decision, but he seems to have supported the view of his company; *The Beggar's Opera* was played, but as a concession to Wilkinson it was agreed 'he might indeed have his Monologue, and a short leading part, as it was for his benefit.'[1]

The same difficulty of a benefit being bespoke is described by Lee Lewes[2] in a strolling company in the 1760's; here there was an additional complication, for the "gentlemen of the hunt" who bespoke the play, conceived themselves to possess also the right to cast it, and allotted to the youthful beneficiary the part of the hero which had been for untold years in the hands of the ageing manager.

The Services were always notable bespeakers of plays apart from their liberal patronage of the benefits of individual players. At a Service bespeak the enthusiasm was always hearty, and the proceedings were quite liable to provide the rest of the audience with an additional element of entertainment. At a naval officers' bespeak in North Shields in 1794 'several songs were sung in the gallery by some of the crew of the *Albacore* and very well received.'[3]

The bigger military garrison towns, of which Dublin was one, continued to enjoy bespeaks by the Regiments stationed there until the rise of the touring system in the later 1870's deprived such functions of their historic point. In 1865 the officers of the 11th Hussars bespoke a play at Dublin[4] and there may well be later instances of regimental bespeaks, though the regimental patronage of individual benefits, more pronounced perhaps when a female beneficiary combined talent with beauty, continued till the end of the 1880s. The sole exception that has been noticed comes from Derby in 1823 when the officers of the cavalry refused to bespeak owing to non-conformist prejudice. The Regiment is not named, but as the British Cavalry later than Cromwell's Ironsides has been more noted for playgoing than non-conformity, one must conceive this as a tactful gesture towards the feelings of the local citizens.[5]

A memoir writer who was the lessee of the Exeter Theatre about 1859, gives a charming indication of the intimate and local nature of some of these performances with the words:

It was no uncommon thing after returning thanks for a bespeak given by some great family, to find the head of it would rise and answer. Such an honour was accorded to me by Sir Stafford

[1] Percy Fitzgerald, *Life of David Garrick*, I, 337, 338.
[2] Charles Lee Lewes, *Memoirs*, London, 1805, I, 55-57.
[3] Robert King, *The Theatres of North Shields*, Gateshead, 1948, p. 25.
[4] *History of the Theatre Royal, Dublin*, p. 168.
[5] Sybil Rosenfeld, *The Theatrical Notebooks of T. H. Wilson Manly*, in *Theatre Notebook*, VII, No. 1 (1952).

Northcote, Mr Nation and other wealthy and influential families.[6]

The heads of great families were not always so considerate, for at Nottingham in 1829 the Earl of Chesterfield, having bespoken a play, forgot to come.[7]

Norwich, Swansea and Perth, as three cities of the second theatrical rank, will provide a representative selection of those corporations, persons and bodies likely to bespeak plays in the period 1830-1840.

Most imposing was the occasion at Norwich in 1839 when, a son succeeding a popular father in the management of the Theatre Royal, he was given a "send off" with bespeaks on three successive nights by the Sheriff, the Mayor, and the High Sheriff of the County.[8] An annual bespeak by the Mayor (called in Swansea the Portreeve) and Corporation was a standing dish, but in the years following the Reform Bill of 1832 when party feeling ran high, there were occasional incidents. At Norwich in 1835, the Mayor, who was a Reformer, refused his bespeak for some reason or other, so the rival party, the Conservatives, quickly organized a "night" of their own, selecting *The Rivals* and Foote's *The Mayor of Garratt*.[9]

At Norwich in the 1770's the Committee running the theatre applied to the Mayor for a bespeak, but in general these corporative bespeaks were spontaneous, in fact almost automatic.

The two Members of Parliament for Norwich could always be relied upon for an annual bespeak[10] and other corporate bodies to which a manager might look for this support were at Norwich the Guardians and the Wine Clubs,[11] and at Swansea the Freemasons (excellent theatre patrons everywhere) and the Tradesmen.[12] The sporting associations were always very forward in this kind of entertainment. Between 1831 and 1839 at Swansea bespeaks came from The Cricket Club, the Archery Club, the Stewards of the Races and the Stewards of the Regatta.[13] At Perth in 1835 the Royal Perth Golfing Society called their bespeak a "grand fashionable night".[14]

[6] Fred Belton, *Random Recollections of An Old Actor*, London, 1880, p. 227.
[7] Sybil Rosenfeld, *The Theatrical Notebooks of T. H. Wilson Manly*, in *Theatre Notebook*, VII, No. 1 (1952).
[8] Bosworth Harcourt, *op. cit.*, p. 30.
[9] *Ibid.*, p. 24, and Cecil Price, *op. cit.*, p. 109.
[10] Bosworth Harcourt, *op. cit.*, p. 20.
[11] *Ibid.*, pp. 38, 39.
[12] Cecil Price, *op. cit.*, p. 109.
[13] *Ibid.*
[14] Peter Baxter, *op. cit.*, p. 226.

IV—THE DATE

THE THEATRICAL SEASON in the 18th and 19th centuries ran from mid-September to July, and the Benefit Season began at first in February. The earlier benefits were considered the more advantageous, before the liberality of playgoers became exhausted.

In the earlier period, from 1680 to about 1720, the Lord Chamberlain (still exercising a semi-paternal rule over the theatres) sometimes decided dubious priorities himself, and in 1719-1720 he issued an order to the Drury Lane managers not to allow any benefits before Mrs Oldfield's and Mrs Porter's.[1]

Though in 1709 Mrs Oldfield's benefit was in February, in 1712 the Lord Chamberlain also laid down 'That no play be acted for the benefit of any Actor before ye first day of March', but this prohibition does not appear to have been effective.[2]

Quite early on managements tried to obviate scrambling and unpleasantness by nominating the benefit months in the artists' contracts. A group of Drury Lane contracts signed in 1709[3] shows clearly the relationship between annual salary and benefit month as follows: Mrs Oldfield, £200—February; Pinkethman and Mills, £100—March; Firbank, 40/- per week—March; Johnson, £100—April; Bowen, £75—April; Husband, £65—April. As so often happened, not only in relation to benefits, prominent singers found themselves in a favoured position, and in 1705 Mrs Tofts, though she only signed her three months contract on January 28, was able to stipulate for a benefit on February 19.[4] Madame Albertazzi did better still in the 1830's, for Alfred Bunn, the manager of Drury Lane, records that she 'having, during the recess, made her debut on the English stage by taking a benefit on the 20th of August at Drury Lane Theatre, was considered, as she proved, a valuable acquisition to it.'[5]

How a stranger without the patronage or connection to "make" a good benefit, however great her Continental reputation, could have

[1] Allardyce Nicoll, *XVIIIth Century Drama 1700-1750*, App. B, p. 284.
[2] *Ibid.*, p. 281.
[3] *Ibid.*, p. 286.
[4] *Ibid.*, p. 290.
[5] Alfred Bunn, *op. cit.*, III, 97.

filled the vast spaces of Drury Lane at the end of August, must remain something of a mystery.

As early benefits proved remunerative, the managers soon attempted to retain these early nights for themselves, pushing the players' benefits into the Spring and Summer months, unless there was any reason to advance them, as when at Covent Garden in 1746-1747 'the season was so bad that in February the benefits commenced.'[6]

The managers naturally wore the players down in the end until custom was established, and by 1814 at Drury Lane there was only one benefit as early as April.[7] But this wearing down process was gradual; in 1774 Spranger Barry could still write to Garrick 'there are but very few benefits after the first week in May, except the lower ones.'[8] There is a second evidence on this point in the memoirs of Everard, who, writing of a period round about 1765, says 'the latter end of Covent Garden season, when scarce any of the first rate actors would play in the month of May, for the door-keepers benefits he (Powell) performed every night in the week for them.'[9]

As late as 1805 Harris apologizes to Munden for fixing his benefit at Covent Garden on May 14—'it is very late to be sure.'[10] The earlier the better remained the rule, and a quite exceptional part of G. F. Cooke's reward for resounding success in his first Covent Garden season 1800-1801 was that his benefit, besides being made "clear", was advanced to January 27.[11]

But Colley Cibber's view of about 1711 that the harvest of the management's gains was over by March[12] altered greatly in the next ninety years, for in the famous Covent Garden dispute of 1800, from which there are so many theatrical details to be learned, an article of complaint was that of the proprietors 'producing new plays during the course of the Benefits.'[13] This implied that the management was subjecting its artists' benefits, from April onwards, to undue competition, and indicated the players' view that poten-

---

[6] Tate Wilkinson, *Memoirs of His Own Life*, III, 185.
[7] Garrick Club Playbill Collection.
[8] *The Private Correspondence of David Garrick*, I, 619.
[9] E. C. Everard, *op. cit.*, p. 9.
[10] *Memoirs of J. S. Munden*, by His Son, London, 1846, p. 197.
[11] William Dunlap, *op. cit.*, I, 138, 139.
[12] Colley Cibber, *op. cit.*, II, 11.
[13] *Statement of Differences subsisting between the Proprietors and Performers of the Theatre Royal Covent Garden, given in the Correspondence which has passed between them*, London, 1800, p. 30.

tially attractive novelties should only be produced in the earlier part of the season, which was, of course, in general the case, as managers would desire to exploit their novelties to the full before the summer break. Priority of benefit date according to salary persisted through the period, though its rigidity weakened towards the end—'a Benefit in Course of Salaries' was a common expression in 18th century contracts. In 1808 when Young was about to pass upwards from the Haymarket to Covent Garden, Colman, his manager at the former theatre, advising him to accept the offer that was to his advantage, wrote:

> He [Harris] wishes you to appear at Covent Garden, with all due honours, beginning from that time on a regular engagement for three years, at the salary of 18 l per week—a benefit each year, of course, being included; which benefit, from your salary, will rank as one of the very earliest ones.[14]

By the beginning of the 19th century in the provinces where so many performers were usually grouped upon the same low salary mark, it seems to have been customary to draw lots for priority of date.

Next to an early benefit, the main desire of the player in London was that the benefit should not fall upon an opera night, when the fashionables who were the hoped-for box patrons would be listening to the Italian singers, though oddly enough in 1702 the Lord Chamberlain had to order that benefits should *not* take place on opera nights.[15] The avoidance of a clash was a touch and go business, for the opera nights were not necessarily known when the season's benefit dates were arranged. Both Mrs Bellamy and Mrs Abington encountered this difficulty, dealing with it in their several ways. Mrs Bellamy quickly exchanged with the next in rank, Mrs Hamilton, who was proud to have *first* benefit, not caring about the opera, 'as her interest did not lie among the box people.'[16] Mrs Abington wanted to have it both ways, and made such a fuss with Garrick that he finally had to take counsel's opinion on her case, this being the occasion on which he called her 'that worst of bad women.'

In 1768 a row blew up at Drury Lane over Mrs Clive's benefit,

---

[14] Julian C. Young, *op. cit.*, I, 52.
[15] Allardyce Nicoll, *XVIIIth Century Drama 1700-1750*, p. 281.
[16] *Life of George Anne Bellamy*, III, 55.

which had been fixed for March 17, a date she refused, both because Mrs Dancer had been announced for an earlier benefit, and because it was St Patrick's Day. Her words were 'I will not accept of that day, nor will I advertise for it.'[17] Mrs Clive did not like St Patrick's Day, which was probably rowdy in 1768, but Tom Dibdin had an even better justified cause of complaint when his Drury Lane benefit in 1823 'was appointed for one of the leading days of Epsom races.' He declined, 'and had another and worse night assigned.'[18] The leading day of Epsom races is a poor night in the West End theatres to the present time. The comedian Munden, who always had a keen eye for business, in his agreement for the season 1820-1821 at Drury Lane, had a cause stipulating that his benefit should not be in Epsom race week.[19] He also barred a Friday or a Saturday. In 1774 Mrs Yates also barred Saturday in her articles with Garrick,[20] which rings oddly now that, within living memory, Saturday has always been the best theatrical night of the week, but half-holidays and early closing had not then been invented.

For the seasons 1834-1835 and 1835-1836 at Drury Lane two contracts survive, those of Macready and Farren. Where Farren stipulated 'to have that benefit early, and a choice of night,' Macready was still more specific; his benefit was to be 'the first without exception' and on a Monday.[21]

Though in general Assize Week vied with Race week, and the weeks of the great seasonal Fairs that had survived from the Middle Ages, as an excellent one for theatricals, even that rule had its exception, and at Perth in 1830 there were complaints of bad benefits in Assize Week as the Courts sat late and the public became quite carried away discussing the trials.[22]

The actual refusal of a benefit date could be a symptom of general disgruntlement, as was very clearly visible when Spranger Barry wrote to Garrick in 1775 'I beg you will not be offended at my not taking a benefit . . . but my friends as well as myself, think me slightly treated in this whole business'—the business being a dispute with Miss Pope over benefit dates.[23]

[17] Percy Fitzgerald, *Life of Mrs Clive*, London, 1888, pp. 70-74.
[18] Thomas Dibdin, *op. cit.*, II, pp. 256, 257.
[19] *Memoirs of J. S. Munden*, p. 282.
[20] *The Private Correspondence of David Garrick*, I, 624.
[21] Alfred Bunn, *op. cit.*, I, pp. 55 (note), 286, 287.
[22] Peter Baxter, *op. cit.*, p. 191.
[23] *The Private Correspondence of David Garrick*, II, 59.

Where clashing was avoidable, there was give and take in genuine cases. In 1775 Garrick even went so far as to alter the date of the Theatrical Fund benefit at Drury Lane on a representation from Miss Macklin, of whom he held a high opinion, that her benefit would be injured, though as she was playing at Covent Garden, she had no real claim on him.[24]

Sometimes an artist had to face the disappointment of postponing a benefit, if the star who had been cajoled to play fell ill, and this might introduce dangerous elements of theatre politics. Mrs Bellamy gives a glimpse of this in her *Life*.[25]

> My illness . . . obliged Mr Ross to postpone his benefit, at which I was to appear in the character of Juliet, and he in Romeo. Mr Garrick, upon this, wished him to change that play for one in which my presence was not necessary. He at the same time hinted to me, that it would be degrading to my consequence to appear with an inferior actor.

Garrick, whose Romeo had not been admired greatly, had every motive to prevent his Juliet appearing with a younger lover of Verona at a benefit.

But to balance these disappointments was the occasional stroke of lucky timing, as when Tate Wilkinson's benefit at Portsmouth in 1758 was packed by the troops and sailors of an expeditionary force that sailed three days later.[26] This was not Wilkinson's only piece of fortunate benefit timing, for when years later he agreed at some inconvenience to postpone his departure from York by twenty-four hours and appear at a benefit for charity children, this led to his being offered the lesseeship of the Theatre Royal in that city and the circuit of adjacent theatres, which he held for close on thirty years.[27] Another to be aided later on his way to success by the opportune timing of a benefit was E. A. Sothern. About 1852 he chanced to be in Birmingham when his old Jersey manager, now again an actor, was taking a benefit there. Sothern was offered a good juvenile part in a farce, scored a hit, and received an engagement from the Birmingham manager.[28]

Mrs Sarah Ward, writing to her lover from Liverpool in 1759

[24] *Ibid.*, II, 53.
[25] *Life of George Anne Bellamy*, II, 168.
[26] Tate Wilkinson, *Memoirs of His Own Life*, I, pp. 195, 196.
[27] *Ibid.*, III, 117.
[28] T. Edgar Pemberton, *op. cit.*, p. 9.

when her benefit had not yet been fixed, said 'The East
India fleet is expected in eight or ten days, which will make
a prodigious alteration in the receipts; I hope I shall stay off
till then.'[29]

Besides a clash with an opera night, another inauspicious event,
to be avoided if possible, was a benefit immediately before or immediately after that of a major star. This disadvantage was magnified
in the Drury Lane and Covent Garden companies in which Mrs
Siddons exercised direct ascendancy after her preliminary successes
in 1783-1785 (correspondingly on her summer provincial tours), and
the jealousy aroused was not diminished by her own arrogant
attitude.

> Her nights of performance alone were well attended, and she
> had two benefits each season, for which everything fashionable
> reserved itself; and the benefits of others, if she did not act for
> them, were reduced nearly to the actor's private connexion, and
> many were disappointed in their little circles by an apology that
> ended with 'You know we *must go* on Mrs Siddons's night, and
> then we leave town directly.'[30]

From Dublin in 1809 Mrs Jordan wrote, not without some satisfaction, 'Kemble's benefit was last night; a very bad house, £250.
This is laid to me.'[31] Yet one further instance in which the sock
proved more rewarding than the buskin. Seven years earlier there is
a note of Kemble himself having caused similar dismay, and the
regular members of the Bath company had complained of very
indifferent support for their benefits, which followed closely upon
Kemble's departure from the city.[32]

The dropping into place of this jig-saw puzzle of the annual
benefits of his company must have been a perpetual headache to the
manager, and one of the causes of complaint of the Covent Garden
actors in 1800 was that notice of their benefit dates had been
reduced from four weeks to three.[33] In the provinces this grievance

[29] *Letters between Mr West Digges and Mrs Sarah Ward, 1752-1759,* Edinburgh, 1833, p. 123.
[30] James Boaden, *Life of Mrs Jordan,* I, 66.
[31] A. Aspinall, *op. cit.,* p. 93.
[32] S. Penley, *op. cit.,* p. 90.
[33] *Statement of Differences subsisting between the Proprietors and Performers
of the Theatre Royal Covent Garden, given in the Correspondence which has
passed between them,* pp. 1, 117.

appears to have been even stronger, only a week's notice of a benefit being given at Bath in 1775.[34]

The right of fixing the benefit date was not infrequently used by managers for the base purpose of evading the obligation entirely. When Everard was playing at Brighton in the Summer of 1776 under the management of Johnstone, son of the Box-book-keeper at Drury Lane, this manager, knowing that the actor was re-engaged for Drury Lane that winter, tried to cheat him by fixing his Brighton benefit for the day he was due at Drury Lane for rehearsals. Remonstrances were unavailing, and time became short, so Everard consulted his friends, and on their advice, went in front one night when he was not playing and addressed the audience from the gallery, putting his case. The audience took his part, called for the manager, and after an exchange of public argument, Johnstone was forced to give Everard a benefit on a date when he could take it.[35] Here is another example from about the same period, also from the ever-aggrieved Everard:

> [Gloucester]—In order to be revenged on me for not continuing, he [the manager] immediately fixed my benefit, not only on the worst night in the week (Friday) but the Wednesday before and the Monday after, he allotted to two performers, who he knew would have overflowing houses, (Shuter and Fox), and that between the two fires it was impossible for me to clear a shilling: that turned out exactly to be the case; I rather lost than gained by it.[36]

The difficulties of benefit allocation could have their disciplinary uses. In 1806 the by then thoroughly demoralized G. F. Cooke was playing at Covent Garden, and Harris was kind enough to release him to play at Bath and Bristol. On his way back he stopped at Marlborough to get drunk for nine days, 'and when he returned to London found that the nights had been assigned for the benefits, and of course no notice taken of him.'[37]

Occasionally even the manager's personal interest had to give way to the general good of the theatre. So we find Mrs Bellamy writing on a note of triumph in her initial success about 1744,

[34] *The Private Correspondence of David Garrick*, II, 45.
[35] E. C. Everard, *op. cit.*, pp. 59-62.
[36] *Ibid.*, pp. 172, 173.
[37] William Dunlap, *op. cit.*, I, 295.

As Mr Rich could not afford, from the receipts of the theatre
to allow me a salary equal to the success I met with, and the
capital parts I performed, he gave me a benefit, free of all
expense, upon one of his *own* nights, in order to prevent discord
in the company.[38]

Wise Mr Rich. This is a reminder that, at least from the time of
Garrick's rise in 1742 onwards, a major star could demand and frequently receive more than one benefit in a season, while the
manager usually took two.

A representative synopsis of the dates of benefits of a patent
theatre in the early 19th century can be gathered from the Drury
Lane benefits of the season 1813-1814, the one in which Edmund
Kean first burst upon the town. Eighteen benefits were taken
between April 2 and July 15, 1814, one in April, seven in May, six in
June and two in July. The newly risen star took his benefit seventh
in order on May 25, and it was not until the end of June that two
benefits were held with joint beneficiaries. Mr Spring, Box-Book and
House-Keeper, took the penultimate benefit in July.[39]

Perhaps the Rules and Regulations of the Royal Marylebone
Theatre in November 1837[40] provide the evidence on benefit dates
least comprehensible to the modern mentality. These Rules provide
as Clause 14 that 'Any person announcing their benefit before the
usual time allowed by the Manager to each performer' shall do so
'under the forfeiture of their engagement and the night so announced.' What a curious glimpse of histrionic indiscipline at a
minor theatre as Queen Victoria was ascending the throne that the
danger of 'any person' distributing unauthorized announcements of
a benefit needed a penal deterrent in the Rules and Regulations.

Date and place usually go together, so mention may be made here
of a custom at the Haymarket, which had a small capacity, that
benefits could on occasions be moved to a larger theatre. When
Colman in 1796 desired to give a benefit for the dependants of John
Palmer (the original Joseph Surface), who had died upon the stage
in Liverpool, he did not consider his own theatre large enough, and
took his company across the road to play at the Opera House.[41]

[38] *Life of George Anne Bellamy,* I, pp. 60, 61.
[39] Garrick Club Playbill Collection.
[40] Copy in the Collection of the late Malcolm Morley.
[41] John Adolphus, *Memoirs of John Bannister, Comedian,* London, 1839,
II, 26.

When the Covent Garden season collapsed unexpectedly in May 1833, the company moved to the Olympic on a commonwealth basis, but for Bartley's benefit, which was also Mrs Bartley's farewell, they returned to Covent Garden for one night.[42] Later the same point occurs as a stipulation in Macready's terms for an engagement at the Haymarket in 1849, which was that he could take his benefit in such larger theatre as he might be able to secure.[43]

By the middle of the 19th century a sort of tradition had arisen that accorded Drury Lane to the more notable veterans of the stage for their farewell benefits, the piece more often than not being *The School for Scandal* with its unrivalled opportunities for a star cast. Macready was the first to take leave from Drury Lane when not actually engaged there. This was in 1851, and he played *Macbeth*, but both Benjamin Webster in 1874 and John Baldwin Buckstone in 1876 were also thus honoured. Both had *The School for Scandal* and in the former of these benefits Charles Surface was played by Charles Mathews the younger at the age of seventy-two.[44]

[42] Playbill in Garrick Club Collection.

[43] *Macready's Diaries,* II, 431.

[44] Clement Scott and Cecil Howard, *Edward Leman Blanchard*, London, 1891, II, pp. 436 and note, 457 and note.

UNLESS THE BENEFIT were expressly declared to be "clear", which is only an abbreviation for "clear of charges", the beneficiary became responsible for the theatre charges of the night, which paid for salaries, lighting, money-takers, stage staff, orchestra, printing and the like. These "charges" were a prior claim on the receipts of the night, and it was only when the "charges" had been deducted that the beneficiary began to obtain the profits, or share these with the manager in whatever may have been the agreed proportion.

These "charges" constantly increased over the years in sympathy with the constant economic phenomenon now known indifferently as the rise in the cost of living or the fall in the purchasing power of money. This phenomenon was always pleaded by managements in extenuation of any move to increase the charges, and it was as despairingly resented by the players as is the rising cost of living by the whole community to-day. It is significant that the point is raised in one of the two very first documents on the benefit system, as the patentees of Drury Lane informed the Lord Chamberlain in 1694: 'and we Observing y^t although ye receipts of late had been lesse than Usuall yett ye Constant & Incident Charges are higher & consequently needfull to be Retrencht.'[1]

In 1709 the Lord Chamberlain ordered that only a deduction of £40 for the night's charges should be allowed,[2] but this order appears to have been disregarded, for a number of Drury Lane contracts signed in that year for five-year periods contain higher charges. The charges were then regulated upon the biblical principle of to him that hath shall be given, for players drawing an annual salary of £100 paid charges of £40, while those receiving under £100 paid charges of £50 for their benefits.[3] A little earlier, in 1701, there is a contract with charges fixed at £30, but this is also unusual as being for a one-year period.[4] At the smaller Lincoln's

---

[1] Allardyce Nicoll, *Restoration Drama 1660-1700*, pp. 330-340.
[2] Allardyce Nicoll, *XVIIIth Century Drama 1700-1750*, App. B, pp. 282, 283.
[3] *Ibid.*, p. 286.
[4] *Ibid.*, p. 286 (k).

Inn Fields Theatre, with a capacity of £170, the charges can be inferred to have been £35 in 1728.[5]

The first flare-up came with a demand by the patentees for a third of the profits of benefits—additional that is to the "charges"—for the use of the Patent, that invaluable piece of parchment that sanctified theatrical monopoly till 1843. Colley Cibber, himself manager of Drury Lane for twenty-three years, seems to have had no doubt of the ill-faith of his predecessors.

> The Patentees observing that the Benefit-Plays of the Actors, towards the latter End of the Season, brought the most crowded Audiences in the Year; began to think their own Interests too much neglected, by these partial Favours of the Town, to their Actors; and therefore judg'd, it would not be impolitick, in such wholesome annual Profits, to have a Fellow-feeling with them. Accordingly, an *Indulto* was laid of one Third, out of the Profits of every Benefit, for the proper Use, and Behoof of the Patent . . .
>
> Now though the Agreements of these united Actors, I am speaking of in 1708, were as yet, only Verbal; yet that made no Difference to the honest Obligation, to keep them; But, as Honour at that time happen'd to have but a loose hold of their Consciences, the Patentees rather chose to give it the slip, and went on with their Work without it. No Actor, therefore, could have his Benefit fix'd, till he had first sign'd a Paper, signifying his voluntary Acceptance of it, upon the, above, Conditions, any Claims from Custom, to the contrary, notwithstanding. Several at first refus'd to sign this Paper; upon which the next in Rank were offer'd on the same Conditions, to come before the Refusers; this smart Expedient got some few of the Fearful the Preference to their Seniors; who, at last, seeing the Time was so short for a present Remedy, and that they must either come into the Boat, or lose their Tide, were forc'd to comply, with what, they, as yet, silently, resented as the severest Injury. In this Situation, therefore, they chose to let the principal Benefits be over, that their Greivances might swell into some Bulk, before they made any Application for Redress to the Lord-Chamberlain; who, upon hearing their general Complaint, ordered the Patentees to shew cause, why their Benefits had

[1] *Theatre Notebook*, VI, No. 1 (1951).

been diminish'd one Third, contrary to the common Usage? The Patentees pleaded the sign'd Agreement, and the Actors Receipts of the other two Thirds, in full Satisfaction. But these were prov'd to have been exacted from them, by the Methods already mentioned. They notwithstanding insist upon them as lawful. But as Law, and Equity do not always agree, they were look'd on as unjust, and arbitrary. Whereupon the Patentees were warn'd at their Peril, to refuse the Actors full Satisfaction.[6]

This passage throws into relief the double motives of these early managers, the desire to be in on a financial good thing mingling with the equally enduring motive of maintaining the economic subjection of the artists.

The Patentees proving unwisely recalcitrant, the Lord Chamberlain had recourse to the ultimate sanction of closing the theatre on June 6, 1709 with the majestic words 'I do therefore for the S[d] Contempt hereby Silence you from further Acting.'[7]

No more was heard of the deduction of one-third of the profits for 'the Use, and Behoof of the Patent,' but there were other complaints of double-dealing by the patentees. In 1707 Mrs Porter complained that at her postponed benefit in May, although half the actors were "out of pay", she had to provide the full £40 charges.[8] This suggestion that the charges were not always wholly genuine is a recurrent one, and was a major cause of the grave dispute at Covent Garden in 1800. There is, however, to be put on the credit side that the charges were adjustable in hard cases, and Cibber's wayward daughter Mrs Charke, writing of about 1726, records 'I was accordingly engaged [by Fielding] at the Haymarket at Four Guineas per Week, with an Indulgence in Point of Charges at my Benefit.'[9]

But though the amount might be flexible, the occasional attempt of a beneficiary to vary the other normal conditions or impose fresh ones of his own, invariably failed. In 1851 when James Anderson held the lease, Macready desired to have Drury Lane for his farewell benefit, a favour that could hardly be refused to the leader of the profession. Anderson asked for the bare expenses of the night,

[6] Colley Cibber, op. cit., Vol. I, pp. 291, 292.
[7] Allardyce Nicoll, XVIIIth Century Drama 1700-1750, pp. 282, 283.
[8] Ibid., p. 291.
[9] A Narrative of the Life of Mrs Charlotte Charke, Written by Herself, London, 1755, ed. 1929, p. 54.

which the Treasurer certified as £170, and agreed to Macready's stipulation to provide his own money-takers and his own box-office representative. But when Macready laid down 'that all the actors and actresses of Drury Lane must be excluded from the front of the theatre on that night', Anderson refused with indignation, whereupon Macready gave way.[10] No one in theatre history except the arrogant Macready would have been capable of demanding his theatre from a struggling, lesser, rival tragedian and simultaneously suggesting that the artists in such a man's company were scum to be kept out with drunks and prostitutes.

Meanwhile the charges moved steadily up, sometimes inspired merely by the rising cost of living after each successive war, sometimes justified by capital expenditure upon the enlargement of a theatre auditorium with a consequent increase in money capacity. Apparently in the sixty years after the Lord Chamberlain "froze" the benefit charges of Drury Lane at £40 in 1709, these had crept up to 60 guineas. Then we are able to detect the very moment of another rise, for in February 1767 Garrick enlarged the theatre to hold three hundred and thirty seven guineas instead of two hundred and twenty, raising the benefit charge from sixty to seventy guineas.[11] In 1780 the Drury Lane charges were £100,[12] in 1800 £160,[13] in 1815 two hundred guineas,[14] in 1823 two hundred and twenty guineas,[15] but the last figure noted for this theatre is £210 in 1834,[16] for the frugal £170 of half-bankrupt Anderson in 1851 was scarcely normal.

At the smaller Haymarket the charges were £63 in 1778, and by 1796 these had risen to £84.[17]

At Covent Garden in 1760 the charges stood at £60,[18] in 1780 at £64;[19] by 1799 they had jumped to £140, and it was their sudden

---

[10] James R. Anderson, *op. cit.*, pp. 192, 193.
[11] R. B. Peake, *op. cit.*, I, pp. 191-193.
[12] Thomas Davies, *op. cit.*, II, 3.
[13] *Statement of Differences subsisting between the Proprietors and Performers of the Theatre Royal Covent Garden, given in the Correspondence which has passed between them*, p. 5.
[14] Thomas Dibdin, *op. cit.*, II, 102.
[15] *Ibid.*, II, 257
[16] *Macready's Diaries*, I, 136.
[17] *Recollections of the Life of John O'Keeffe*, I, 366, II, 346.
[18] Tate Wilkinson, *Memoirs of His Own Life*, III, 173.
[19] *Statement of Differences subsisting between the Proprietors and Performers of the Theatre Royal Covent Garden, given in the Correspondence which has passed between them*, p. 26.

raising by Thomas Harris to £160 in 1800 that precipitated the conflict with his principal actors, with an accompanying pamphlet war
that gives us valuable inner details of the charges and the benefit
system in general at the junction of the centuries. This dispute must
now be considered.

The performers describe the increase by £20 as unreasonable, as
salaries had not risen proportionately to charges since 1780. When
Harris gave them an assurance, supported by a declaration from his
Treasurer, that the nightly expenses were in fact over £160, they
asked to see the details and were refused. So they tackled the figures
for themselves. They pointed out that in a season averaging one
hundred and ninety-two acting nights, nightly expenses of £160
would make the total expenses of the season £30,720. But as the
annual salaries of the ten principal performers together only
amounted to £3,205, or just over ten per cent of the expenses, they
had difficulty in believing Harris's figures, salaries being always 'a
very great proportion of theatrical disbursements.'[20]

The manager then shifted his ground, urging that 'the enlargement of the Theatre, and the advancement of the prices is more
than an equivalent for the unavoidable increased charge of the
Benefits.' And he added that he had spent £40,000 on new scenery
and clothes during his management. The rejoinder of the players
upon these two points was of unequal merit, for their contention
that if the public were fools enough to pay increased prices, that
was no concern of theirs, carried less weight than their plaintive
reminder that they were not allowed to have the plays with new
scenery at their benefits, only old ones.[21]

Though this was the position with regard to new plays at Covent
Garden in 1800, managements had two alternative methods at the
end of the 18th century of protecting any specially cherished novelty
of the season from a depreciation of its attractiveness by constant
repetition at benefits as well as on stock nights. They could, as has
just been seen, impose the managerial veto on the composition of
the benefit bill, or they could charge the beneficiary a premium for
the use of such a piece at his benefit. A successful working dramatist,
Charles Dibdin, provides the evidence.

In fact the opera [*A Christmas Tale*], had most capital success,
and was, indeed, such a favourite, that the performers gave

[20] *Ibid.*, pp. 4, 5, 13, 25, 26.
[21] *Ibid.*, pp. 27, 29, 30.

twenty guineas, in addition to the usual expences, to be permitted to have it for the benefits.[22]

The fact was that, in spite of increased theatre capacities, the proportionate increase of charges was disadvantageous to the actor, and the point was well put, about 1800, after the rebuilding of Drury Lane between 1791 and 1794, by old Charles Bannister, who had played with Garrick.

Mr Garrick's theatre held, when well filled, something less than three hundred and fifty pounds; other theatres [he means the new theatre] would contain between six and seven hundred; but the difference in a benefit was very great indeed. Mr Garrick's curtain drew up at an expense of sixty pounds at the most; and if I came forward in a new character, or even advertised a new song, it would fill the house, and I should put nearly three hundred pounds into my pocket. In after times the first two hundred guineas that were received went to pay expenses; in order to gain that and a surplus, I was obliged to depend on my personal influence, and consequently to frequent clubs and live in taverns, a practice expensive in itself, and of bad consequence as a habit.[23]

The Drury Lane building that Bannister is speaking of had a maximum money capacity of £826 and could 'conveniently admit within its walls a nightly receipt of £700,'[24] so he is justified in saying 'six or seven hundred', and though in practice anything over £450 was a very good benefit indeed in that theatre, his main point is valid.

[22] The Professional Life of Mr Dibdin, Written by Himself, Dublin, 1791, I, 108.

[23] John Adolphus, op. cit., II, 64.

[24] James Boaden, Life of Mrs Jordan, London, 1831, I, 252, II, 309.

VI—PROFITS AND LOSSES

THE BENEFIT CARRIED WITH IT of necessity rather more of the element of gambling than merely that inherent in the entertainment business, for the player lacked the manager's ability to recoup poor nights by later good ones. A bad benefit meant a bad season financially, and English weather was as unkind and unpredictable in the benefit period as now. An active, intelligent and popular artist could, it is true, effect a certain measure of insurance against Fate in various ways. A benefit-bill that contained some striking attraction, such as the unusual casting of a favourite play, would bring playgoers through snow and slush. Tickets sold in advance to personal patrons, provided that there had been a sale rather than a promise, were immune from cancellation, and the "gold tickets" or the "guineas" of personal presents could make up a considerable sum to supplement the sale of tickets and takings at the doors.

The first notably successful benefit was that on Betterton's retirement in 1709 when 'the Town paid a particular deference to him by making his day worth 500 l.'[1]

The most profitable benefit of the 18th century was almost certainly one taken by Mrs Bellamy by which she claimed to have cleared 'upwards of eleven hundred pounds,'[2] at a time when the normal money capacity of the theatre concerned would have been about £200-£220. This might be considered one of her many tall stories, were it not for her frank admission that she was at that time under the "protection" of Mr Fox, the Secretary at War, and 'all the military gentlemen, therefore, seized this opportunity to court my favour'—with one eye on their prospects of promotion.

But these extraneous aids to a satisfactory benefit could be double-edged, for upon another occasion Mrs Bellamy found her benefit "emoluments" greatly reduced, as 'the gentlemen were kept at a

[1] Charles Gildon, *Life of Thomas Betterton,* London, 1710, p.11.
The account in No. 1 of *The Tatler* puts this benefit in a slightly different light. It was a "two-thirds" benefit after payment of charges, and yielded as such £76-4-5, 'but by his tickets, the lowest at half a guinea . . . it is thought he cleared at least £450, over and besides the £76-4-5'.
[2] *Life of George Anne Bellamy,* II, 199, 200.

distance by a belief that Mr Metham was a favoured lover,'[3]—a belief, it may be said, which was entirely correct.

Colley Cibber states[4] that during his managerial regime at Drury Lane (1710-1733), Mrs Oldfield's benefits were averaging £600, which is a high figure for this time.

A popular actress, if not too strait-laced in her attitude, might also hope for such a windfall as came to Mrs Jordan on one of her "nights", forty years or so later, when, according to contemporary gossip, 'she received a purse of three hundred pounds from the club at Brooke's.' But in fairness to the lady it must be added that her official biographer regards this purse as a tribute from the Whig club to the mistress of a Royal Duke of Whig opinions—all the sons of George III counting as Whigs by reason of their opposition to their Tory parent.[5]

For his two benefits at Drury Lane in 1805 Master Betty received £2,540.[6] But so quickly did the vogue of the Young Roscius collapse that his London benefit in February 1806 brought only £309.[7] In his great year of 1805, however, he also secured his future by several triumphal tours, and at Newcastle, where the average nightly receipts of the theatre were £145, his benefit fetched £213, which stood as a box-office record for some years.[8]

There are two most revealing sets of figures, in date just under a hundred years apart, that show the relationship of the average benefit to the salary of the beneficiary among leading performers, and these are sufficiently valuable to be set out in detail. The first figures, which relate to Drury Lane in 1708-1709, have the additional advantage of including an estimate by the theatre Treasurer of the amount of "guineas", or personal presents, received in addition to

---

[3] *Ibid.*, II, 38.

[4] Colley Cibber, *op. cit.*, I, 295.

[5] *Life of George Anne Bellamy*, III, 59, quoting *Secret History of the Green Room*, and George Boaden, *Life of Mrs. Jordan*, I, 84.

[6] S. M. Ellis, *Life of Michael Kelly*, London, 1930, p. 372.

[7] James Boaden, *Life of Mrs. Jordan*, I, 201.

[8] Harold Oswald, *The Theatres Royal in Newcastle upon Tyne*, Newcastle, 1936, p. 55.

the profits of the house.[9] The second figures are those for Covent Garden in the season 1798-1799.[10] For purposes of comparison a point to be taken into account is that the Drury Lane season at the earlier date was of 135 acting nights, that of Covent Garden at the later date 192 nights. The figures given are in both cases net benefit figures; the "charges" of £40 have already been deducted in the Drury Lane document, while the writer has made a corresponding deduction of £120 in the Covent Garden figures.

Drury Lane 1708-9

Actor or Actress	Salary	Benefit	"Guineas"*	Total Benefit
Mr Wilks	168	90	40	130
Mr and Mrs Betterton	112	76	450	526
(His farewell benefit)				
Mr Eastcourt	112	51	200	251
Mr Cibber	112	51	50	101
Mr and Mrs Mills	112	58	20	78
Mrs Oldfield	56	62	120	182
(only played 14 weeks)				

Covent Garden 1798-9

Actor or Actress	Salary	Benefit	"Guineas"*	Total Benefit
Mr Incledon	413	499	—	499
Mr Holman	380	230	—	230
Mr Pope	380	215	—	215
Mrs Pope	254	271	—	271
Mr Munden	380	510	—	510
Mr Fawcett	380	412	—	412
Mr H Johnston	380	214	—	214
Mr J Johnstone	318	358	—	358
Mr Knight	318	272	—	272

* The figures in this column are an estimate in pounds of what the "guineas" roughly brought in. V.C.C-B.

[9] John Williams ("Anthony Pasquin"), *The Eccentricities of John Edwin*, London, 1791, I, 219-224.

It is not satisfactory that a long document dealing with conditions in 1708-1709, and purporting to be signed by the Treasurer of Drury Lane, Zachary Briggs, should only be known from its inappropriate insertion in a book of jokes and anecdotes of a comedian, published by a writer of bad repute in 1791. But the authenticity of the document does not seem to have been challenged since that time, and there seems no reason why Pasquin should have inserted a forged document in his book, though he was capable of anything.

[10] *Statement of Differences subsisting between the Proprietors and Performers of the Theatre Royal Covent Garden, given in the Correspondence which has passed between them*, p. 18.

Some beneficiaries opted for honour and glory rather than cash. When John Bannister, in the summer of 1799, was invited to play for a few weeks plus a benefit at Weymouth, the seaside resort favoured by George III, 'he declined remuneration, saying he deemed the honour sufficient.' The King patronized what still seems to have been announced as his "benefit"—a somewhat hollow compliment—and also invited him sailing on the Royal yacht.[11]

But none the less the possibility of loss remained an ever present one, especially to lesser players who might too rashly brave the hazards of a benefit, and in the days when all actors understood enough dog-Latin to make mild jokes in that language—an example comes from Dublin in 1764—a bad benefit was sourly known as a *malefit*.[12] Even Mrs Jordan at the height of her fame lost £25 on her benefit at Liverpool in 1809 on a very wet night,[13] which would represent a mountain of debt to a lesser player with a wife and family.

The fluctuations that made benefits a real game of hazard are best understood when either the money capacity of the theatre or the average nightly takings of the season are known. During Austin and Whitlock's management of the Theatre Royal, Newcastle in the season 1786-1787, the average receipts per acting night were £41, with the best benefit, that of Mrs Whitlock the wife of the manager, £76, and the lowest benefit £8-15-0.[14]

In general a newcomer to a provincial company was often reluctant to face the risk of a benefit loss, especially if he felt his new colleagues to be hostile, and these considerations are well set out by the unfortunate Everard:

> I had been scarcely a month there [Leicester] before they had to throw, as was customary, for the benefits. I wished to decline, alleging the short time I had been in the company, and that there was no partner to go with me, and a single benefit, which I had always before, was, in this company, on no account allowed; then being told that the nights were all fixed, and that I could possibly have no other chance, at last reluctantly I consented, and, as ill chance would have it, won the first night. As I had purposely been lain on the shelf, a little vanity, more than

---

[11] John Adolphus, *op. cit.*, II, 50.
[12] *Recollections of the Life of John O'Keeffe*, Written by Himself, I, 59.
[13] A. Aspinall, *op. cit.*, p. 109.
[14] Harold Oswald, *op. cit.*, p. 8.

hopes of gain, urged me on to the venture; the trouble and any additional expense I knew must be all my own, and, if there should be any profit, I had to share it with an undeserving set. I therefore took no pains about it. I flattered myself that I should have an opportunity of shewing myself to some advantage, which in the end might answer some end, and that I should have the secret satisfaction of mortifying them a little in my turn. As I foresaw, so it fell out: there was hardly the bare nightly charges.[15]

The same 'unfortunate son of Thespis' later encountered another not unusual misfortune, the illness of a star with its resultant prospect of loss. This customarily led to an attempt to postpone, which in turn might frequently lead to a dispute between performer and manager with mutual accusations of bad faith. Where the manager had received the charges in advance, or taken security for them, he had the whip hand. Here is the normal course of such a dispute from Brighton in 1778, where the charges were £20.

In the morning of the play-day, I had given him my note of hand for the same [i.e. charges], as was customary with all. In the afternoon Mrs Baddeley was suddenly taken so dangerously ill, that it was impossible for her to play. This to me was a thunder-stroke! What could I do? I was in the lion's paw! The manager told me I must do some other play. I replied 'Let me do what I will, there won't be three pounds in the house.' 'I can't help that,' says he, 'I won't lose the night.' 'Well,' said I, warmly, 'I won't come near the theatre; you can't force me to play.' 'No,' rejoined he, 'I can't force you to play, nor you can't force me to shut up my house; I shall have the theatre lighted up as usual: the company will all be here; I shall keep the doors open from six till twelve; if you don't come, I have got your note for twenty pounds, payable on demand; I shall send my treasurer to you with it early tomorrow morning, and if you don't immediately take it up, I'll arrest you for it.' — (Pleasant enough that) — He then went on—'On the other hand, if you will settle some play, and do the best you can with the night, I'll never distress you about your note, and soon as possible you shall have another benefit.' After a short consultation with a few friends, I was advised 'of two evils take the least', and the

15 E. C. Everard, *op. cit.*, p. 111.

last. I accordingly performed the *Stratagem,* had about ten pounds in tickets in the house, and not two in cash; in fine . . . I was twelve pounds loser by the night. The manager 'tis true, kept his word to me, by not distressing me for the balance of my note; he only stopped every shilling of my salary till it was paid, without the least allowance or abatement, and then generously, as he had promised, let me have another benefit for another twenty pounds, and by which, 'tis true, I might have cleared twenty more, but the loss of the first reduced the profits of the second to a very small remuneration.[16]

Charles Mathews the elder, fulfilling his first engagement at the age of seventeen at Dublin in 1794 at a salary of a guinea a week, wrote home to a friend, 'I am not obliged to take "a benefit". Daly deducts money for a benefit from all those who are engaged at the playhouse pay [i.e. payment only for nights of performance]. I am therefore equally well situated with those who have three pounds.'[17] Daly's form of instalment plan insurance that his charges would be forthcoming is of interest. As the Dublin theatre had a capacity of £350 at this time, the charges would have been £50 to £60, and since Mathews only a few weeks earlier, on appearing as a lover in a red coat too small for him, had been greeted by the Dublin gallery with 'A groan for the long lobster', he was indeed fortunate in evading his benefit obligation. Another wretched novice, in the company of a lesser provincial manager named Dunn, said that 'Mr Dunn compelled him to take four benefits a year; he therefore considered that he paid Mr D one shilling and ten-pence per week for acting under his management.'[18]

Sixty-seven years earlier than Mathews, in April 1726, a Mr Wasted, either an unpopular or a very unimportant actor, had had a similar lucky escape at Lincoln's Inn Fields when, his benefit drawing a house of under £20, the audience was, by the custom of that early date, "dismissed", and he avoided having to pay the balance on charges of £35.[19] This gambit of "dismissing" could be made use of deliberately by the shrewd and not over scrupulous, though it was a dangerous and unpopular measure at a benefit. At

---

[16] *Ibid.,* p. 72.

[17] Mrs Mathews, *Memoirs of Charles Mathews, Comedian,* London, 1838, I, 90, 105, quoting letter dated June 23, 1794.

[18] Thomas Leman Rede, *The Road to the Stage,* London, 1827, p. 66.

[19] John Rich's MS Register of performances at Lincoln's Inn Fields Theatre, 1723-1740, in possession of the Garrick Club.

Thomas Sheridan's benefit at Dublin in 1746, a year in which there had been theatre rioting, there was only £10 in the house at seven o'clock, so he took upon himself to "dismiss', ostensibly because of the absence of one actor, though Spranger Barry had rather maliciously offered to read the part.

> This occasioned a pleasant scene, for immediately a terrible "Row" ensued, between the few who paid ready money and those who brought in his benefit tickets. The doorkeepers, not being able to distinguish the real proprietors of the cash, would not refund a penny to either party. After some cuffs and blows, the doors were shut in a great hurry, and all parties dispersed with great dissatisfaction.[20]

An obvious truth in the balance sheet of profit and loss that is rather apt to be overlooked is that when the performer had a bad benefit, the manager almost always had one too, though to a lesser extent since he commandeered such receipts as there might be towards his charges, and had also a lien on the performer's future salary that was probably in the average of a managerial lifetime more theoretical than strictly enforcable when salaries were so near to the subsistence level that a heavily indebted player would naturally rather sneak away than starve.

Tate Wilkinson, who congratulated himself on never taking more than half of the gross receipts of the house on his own benefits, sang rather a different tune a year later in 1785 when other people's benefits were in question, and then the managerial standpoint was uppermost.

> Though it is true on my scheme of the Hull York and Leeds, [theatres] I take half the receipts on benefit-nights, after *my* deducting 4 l or 5 l yet only a few of these benefits are great, many what may be termed decent, and a great many very indecent . . . by the share of a middling house, I barely receive my expenses, and by my share of a bad benefit-night, am in too great a truth a considerable loser.[21]

This would seem to apply to "half benefits" when profits were shared with the manager.

But although Tate Wilkinson grumbled at the possibility of the

[20] *The Private Correspondence of David Garrick*, I, 41, 42.
[21] Tate Wilkinson, *The Wandering Patentee*, II, 226.

manager incurring a loss by a benefit performance, it was John Jackson, manager of the Edinburgh theatre at about the same time, who found the solution to this dilemma by the aid of a wife playing in the company.

> So sensible of this [possibility of a manager losing by a benefit] were Mr King, Miss Farren, Mrs Pope, and Mrs Esten, that in return, they made a voluntary compliment of their performance for Mrs Jackson, which threw something in towards the pecuniary balance in my favour.[22]

No doubt the balance was also tipped in Mr Jackson's favour by an equally voluntary desire of the stars concerned to obtain future engagements at Edinburgh.

The pessimistic view of a benefit—that the recipient was lucky if he escaped with a small loss—endured, according to temperament and circumstances, so long as the benefit system itself. It is to be met with in the late 1880's in a lesser known book by Jerome K. Jerome, author of *Three Men in a Boat,* dealing with his brief career as an actor.

> We are each of us to have a 'ben' before leaving here. I was rather pleased with this when I heard it, but the others displayed no rapture. Our walking gent told me he never lost less than thirty shillings at his benefits. I don't think I shall take one. You pay all expenses and have half the receipts. The attraction about it to my mind, though, is that you can put up what you like, and choose your own parts. I should like to have a try at Romeo.[23]

Though on the whole the more puritanically minded avoided the theatre altogether as the Devil's house, yet in the restricted circle of a provincial city or town, the personal reputation of the beneficiary had a more important influence on the benefit receipt than in the vast and impersonal metropolis. The moral climate varied considerably from city to city, and that of Edinburgh was bleak. 'Mrs Bulkley, notwithstanding her great merits as an actress, was a considerable loser by the night intended for her benefit; I am hurt to say that it might, perhaps, be attributed to her private character falling short of the public estimation.'[24]

[22] John Jackson, *History of the Scottish Stage,* Edinburgh, 1793, pp. 132, 133.
[23] Jerome K. Jerome, *On the Stage, and Off,* London, n.d. [1892] p. 138.
[24] E. C. Everard, *op. cit.,* p. 127.

In rather similar fashion an audience could revenge itself for slights, and Bunn in his memoirs mentions an actor, Sowerby, who in the 1820's had offended the Manchester public by displays of drunkenness, and they punished him by refraining from giving their patronage to his benefit, there being nobody at all in the gallery.[25]

The unhappiest record in respect of the losing benefit would appear to be held by the silver-tongued Charles Murray, afterwards so popular at Covent Garden, for when he and his wife took a benefit at Bath in 1785, they did not sell a single ticket.[26] A close competitor for this booby prize would be Miss Jones's benefit, with the beneficiary playing Rosalind, at Birmingham in 1862, for the pit money-taker reported 'when the doors were opened, there was not a Soul at Pit or Gallery for several minutes.'[27]

Another disastrous benefit was one taken by Tate Wilkinson during an odd, brief season at Birmingham in the 1780 period: 'my receipt was seven pounds! — Not one place taken in the boxes.'[28] At Buxton in 1807 'Mr Hill, from the Bath and Covent Garden Theatres, had not *two* in the house for his benefit and his wife's.'[29] Mr Hill's qualifications should have been sufficient for a spa in Derbyshire, but the actor's position at the theatres mentioned may well have been a modest one. At Brighton in 1843 Mrs Law's benefit had not more than twenty persons present. The money was returned, and the house closed,[30] but the years 1840 to 1844 were very bad theatrically everywhere.

There are instances of a benefit being refused if the beneficiary feared a loss. Indeed, that same Charles Murray, when at Covent Garden twelve years later, possibly deterred by his Bath experience, declined a benefit, and was granted in exchange by Harris the manager the sum of £30, which his fellow players declared to be niggardly.[31] But the most famous refusal, which was that of Mrs Abington in 1776, was less for fear of loss than from pique when the lady found that her benefit coincided with an opera night. If

---

[25] Alfred Bunn, *op. cit.*, II, 307.
[26] *Dictionary of National Biography* (s.v. Charles Murray), quoting Genest.
[27] J. E. Cunningham, *Theatre Royal, Birmingham*, Oxford, 1950, p. 44.
[28] Tate Wilkinson, *The Wandering Patentee*, II, 69.
[29] E. C. Everard, *op. cit.*, p. 232.
[30] H. C. Porter, *op. cit.*, p. 80.
[31] *Statement of Differences subsisting between the Proprietors and Performers of the Theatre Royal Covent Garden, given in the Correspondence which has passed between them*, p. 39.

the star was important enough, some compromise was found, in this case the acceptance of another date provided that Garrick played for her, which he did on the untruthful assurance from Mrs Abington that she was retiring from the stage at the end of the season.[32] It has been suggested that it was her intention to distract public interest from the greater retirement, that of Garrick himself, that season.[33]

A manager anxious to avoid his obligations to concede a benefit night, might make use of the argument of loss, and Garrick, when Tate Wilkinson approached him in 1759 to fix his benefit night, pretended at first that it would not be right to allow a novice to incur the dangerous expenses of a benefit, or at least, unless he were joined with some other artist. Wilkinson had to stand very firm upon the benefit clause in his contract before the date was fixed.[34] A managerial trick of similar intent was played on Charles Dibdin the elder at Covent Garden about 1763. He was gravely informed that if he desired to take a benefit, he must first pay the entire charges into the treasury. Dibdin, being a man of spirit, also stood firmly upon his contract, which contained no such clause, until the management gave way.[35] As will be seen in a later chapter dealing with the settlement after a benefit, what started as a trick became in just over sixty years a contractual device by which a manager insured himself against the actor unable or unwilling to meet the balance of charges in the case of a losing benefit.

Where there had been a dispute ending in the dismissal or withdrawal of a performer, the question of his benefit, a valuable consideration in itself and one that had been taken into account in the fixing of his salary, would arise. The manager usually got the best of such disputes, especially in the early part of the 19th century, as he would be able to plead the breach either of the contract itself by the performer, or the breach of one of the many rules of the theatre that carried with them a managerial right to consider the performer's contract voided. Sometimes the performer might bluff as did Macready when, four days after assaulting Alfred Bunn the manager of the theatre in his office, he wrote to the Drury Lane stage-manager about arrangements for his benefit.[36]

[32] *Life of Mrs Abington*, London, 1888, pp. 81-84.
[33] Percy Fitzgerald, *Life of David Garrick*, II, 378.
[34] Tate Wilkinson, *Memoirs of His Own Life*, I, pp. 272-281.
[35] *The Professional Life of Mr Dibdin*, I, 66-68.
[36] Alfred Bunn, *op. cit.*, II, 39.

Later the position with regard to the refusal of benefits was regularized. Miss Helen Faucit's Covent Garden contract in 1837 contained the clause that she should have a benefit 'in case she should deem it to her advantage,'[37] and this form of clause, putting the benefit at the actor's option, obviated most of the former occasions of dispute.

Benefit losers could hit back if the combination of their London standing and their temporary anger were sufficient for them to damn the possible consequences. Shuter had a bad benefit in Bristol in 1783.

> The next day he took a handful of his neglected night's bills, and walking in the midst of a principal street, strewed them about, crying "Chuck, chuck, chuck!" (the term used in feeding their swine). This bold experiment on their pride and generosity proved successful. Shuter was induced to try a second night, and the house was filled up to the ceiling.[38]

A few later benefit gross receipts for London, when considered with the various figures for the 18th century already given, will tend to show that the rising charges so bitterly complained of, did in fact go *pari passu* with increased receipts for the beneficiary, partly owing to the increasing size of theatres after 1808-1809, and partly owing to a modest rise in the price of theatre seats, mostly in the period 1820-1840.

In the season 1790-1791, Mrs Siddons had a benefit of £412 in Garrick's Drury Lane (pulled down in the latter year), which was considered to hold £337 at normal prices.[39] George Frederick Cooke's benefit in the first flood tide of his success at Covent Garden in the season 1800-1801 was £560—and it was "clear".[40] William Charles Macready's farewell benefit at Drury Lane in 1851 grossed £906, with charges of £170.[41] Paul Bedford, a popular low comedian, taking his departure at the Queens in 1868, received about £700 "including presents of money".[42] Benjamin Webster, veteran manager of the Haymarket and Adelphi, had a farewell benefit at

---

[37] *Macready's Diaries*, I, 405 note (London, 1912).

[38] John Bernard, *Retrospections of the Stage*, London, 1830, II, 16.

[39] James Boaden, *Life of Mrs Siddons*, London, 2nd ed. 1827, II, 287.

[40] Walter Beyham, *The Glasgow Stage*, Glasgow, 1892, p. 61.

[41] Clement Scott and Cecil Howard, *op. cit.*, I, 80, and James R. Anderson, *op. cit.*, pp. 192, 193.

[42] Clement Scott and Cecil Howard, *op. cit.*, II, 360 and note. This is a late date for "presents of money".

Drury Lane in 1874—the conventional all-star *School for Scandal*—which grossed £2,000.[43] Other larger gross figures followed later, but these were more in the nature of charity benefits, and will be considered as such.

---

[43] *Ibid.*, II, 436 and note.

THOUGH THE BENEFITS OF THE MEMBERS of a provincial stock company, as opposed to strollers, who adopted mainly a commonwealth organization, operated in the normal manner of the system as described, there are some points to be noted in connection with the visits during the season of perambulating metropolitan and other stars. Stars actually engaged at Drury Lane or Covent Garden reaped their provincial harvest during the summer months while the Patent Theatres were closed — it was remunerative, though some preferred their comforts and remained in Town to play at the Haymarket — but there were also stars who for one reason or another had no metropolitan engagement during a particular season, and were available to tour all the year round. The constant comings and goings of these strangers, who skimmed the cream off the limited provincial benefit milk, must have been very galling to the members of the stock company, but they knew what they were in for when they engaged. Amongst themselves the stock company had enough domestic heartburnings over benefits. Walter Donaldson, an old actor writing in the 1860's, says sadly 'It has always been acknowledged among actors that benefits in provincial theatres have ever been the source of discord, envy and eternal hatred.'[1] S. W. Ryley says[2] that a 'good benefit maker' was always an object of jealousy, and claims that he was refused an engagement at Manchester in the early 1790's on the grounds of 'my strong benefit interest, which injured the performers who came either before or after me.' It was said expressively of the actor Rayner in the 1830's that he could make a benefit upon Salisbury Plain.

But the respected stock company player or manager could do well, in spite of competition from stars, and when Macready's father was given a final benefit at Birmingham in 1809, 'from one club a purse was made up by each member paying a guinea for his ticket.'[3] By the 1850's a provincial manager who had conducted himself well was treated with even greater formality. After eleven years residence in

---

[1] Walter Donaldson, *Recollections of an Actor*, London, 1865, p. 252.
[2] S. W. Ryley, *The Itinerant*, London, 1817, 3 vol. ed., I, 255.
[3] W. C. Macready, *Reminiscences*, I, 30.

Exeter, Fred Belton was given a "presentation"—no doubt at his farewell benefit, though the occasion is not specifically mentioned as a benefit.

> Three public meetings were held in the Guildhall, duly announced in the papers, and when the subscription list was filled, it bore the best names from the highest to the lowest . . . Mr Head, thrice mayor of Exeter, handed me the presentation, and on that memorable night I was surrounded by the mayor and many members of the corporation, all as if picked—grey headed and grey bearded men of character and position.[4]

Where a provincial circuit was concerned, the benefits could add up to quite a substantial sum if an annual benefit were taken in perhaps each of seven towns. Married couples were still better off; on Mrs Baker's Kent circuit in 1798 Tom Dibdin took two benefits in each town, one as an actor and another as the scene-painter of the company, while his wife took a third.[5] When T. H. Wilson Manly was managing the Nottingham circuit in the year 1821, he took benefits in five towns, and his wife also in five towns, four being the same in each case.[6] In cases where there was no definite circuit, but only a group of minor seaside resorts visited irregularly by the company, other arrangements were made. In the 1770's at Exeter Everard was engaged 'at a guinea and a half a week all the year round, and four single benefits.'[7] Even individual benefits in the provinces could reach huge figures. When the most famous of pantomimes, *Mother Goose,* reached Dublin in 1809, three years after its London production, the benefit of Bradbury the Clown drew £560 and that of Ellar, the Harlequin, £430.[8]

The star played an engagement of from four to ten nights, sometimes even more, plus a benefit in the larger provincial towns—any one or two night stands at lesser towns that were fitted into the touring itinerary did not usually qualify for a benefit. But when Mrs Jordan played at Bath and Bristol in 1809 from April 11 to May 1, she received three benefits,[9] and players visiting Dublin

[4] Fred Belton, *op. cit.,* p. 244.
[5] Thomas Dibdin, *op. cit.,* I, 203.
[6] Sybil Rosenfeld, *The Theatrical Notebooks of T. H. Wilson Manly,* in *Theatre Notebook,* VII, No. 1 (1952).
[7] E. C. Everard, *op. cit.,* p. 69.
[8] Walter Donaldson, *op. cit.,* p. 160.
[9] A. Aspinall, *op. cit.,* p. 82.

appear to have taken two benefits habitually. Star visits were more often on sharing terms than on a "certainty", the star receiving probably "an entire half of the House",[10] or rather less except for the really big names, while the benefit was either "clear", "half clear"[11] or subject to the normal charges, according to the attraction and negotiating skill of the visitor.

There are records of a very great variety of other benefit terms for the provincial visits of London actors, of which the following will give a representative idea of the more usual changes that could be rung. To consider first London artists prepared to play in the provinces for a whole season, West Digges and Mrs Ward, who were living together at the time, were offered a joint engagement at Newcastle in 1759 to play for nine months 'and six benefits.'[12] These were good terms, since one or other of them would be profiting from a benefit every six weeks. John Bannister was offered an alternative at Birmingham in 1800, either 'on Mrs Siddons's or Mr Kemble's terms, viz. to share after forty five guineas, and pay forty five guineas for your benefit the last night of your performing; or, if you prefer taking a clear benefit for the fortnight, (eight nights), 'tis at your service.'[13] The Birmingham capacity being about £250, the former alternative seems the more advantageous, unless business was very bad on stock nights. At Manchester in 1809 the position was unusual, for the theatre was then managed by Elliston, himself a star actor of higher standing than Bannister. He offered to share the benefit house equally with his visitor, he himself also playing in a play containing two good men's parts, *The Beaux Stratagem*.[14]

Between 1830 and 1880 there were also several actors, on the whole of the old classical school, whose appearances in London were only occasional and then often unremunerative, but who were undoubted provincial stars of the first magnitude with an enormous and faithful following, especially in particular cities, where their benefit figures would surpass those of the more genuine London star

[10] *Ibid.*, pp. 50, 51.
[11] W. C. Macready, *Reminiscences*, I, 310.
A "half clear" benefit, in one of the less usual meanings of "half clear", appears to be the explanation of Macready's benefit charges at Birmingham being only £26-10.
[12] *Letters between Mr West Digges and Mrs Sarah Ward, 1752-1759*, Edinburgh, 1833, p. 141.
[13] John Adolphus, *op. cit.*, II, 60.
[14] *Ibid.*, II, 188.

visitors. Three of the leaders of this class were Gustavus Vaughan Brooke, Charles Dillon and Barry Sullivan. Naturally there were variations also in their benefit terms, but they are quite well represented by Gus Brooke's farewell benefit at Belfast, his home town, in 1866, when he 'received half the receipts, taking only a third on other nights.'[15]

Provincial benefit charges seem to have followed London in the main, judged by the ratio between changes and the capacity of the house. Variations are attributable to the rise or decline in importance of certain cities in the last hundred years, and perhaps also to the periodic ups and downs in repute of the theatres concerned, according to the standing of the manager at the time. A table giving some provincial benefit charges at different periods is appended at the end of this chapter.

At Norwich in 1776 the Committee conducting the Theatre Royal offered the artists a curious choice. This was that either the charges should be raised from 20 guineas to 25 guineas, or that during the benefit season there should be four benefits per week instead of three, these being regarded apparently as equivalent advantages to the management. But there seems to have been a protest, for the order was withdrawn.

Information from Liverpool in 1821[16] shows that stars had extra expenses to meet besides the actual "charges". There was a bill for additional properties that might reach £10, and extra advertising and printing averaged £8. This account ends with the sinister item, 'The loss on the collection of ticket money may be fairly estimated at £5.'

In spite of the fact that the star was somewhat at the mercy of the provincial manager over the details of expenses, these provincial benefit figures show that the fatigues of touring by coach were amply compensated by the personal benefit superimposed upon the normal sharing of the receipts.

As far back as Colley Cibber's days at Drury Lane there had been complaint of the "abatement of the Receipts" on the days after a benefit, so the custom was evolved that, to prevent the provincial manager being left too flat and in compensation for the personal gain of the benefit, the star took his or her benefit upon the

[15] W. J. Lawrence, *Life of Gustavus Vaughan Brooke*, Belfast, 1892, pp. 262, 263.
[16] *Liverpool Theatrical Investigator*, I, 58, 158, 488.

penultimate night of the visit, and played the last night "for the Theatre" without salary.

When the star was suspicious of the theatre capacity or the philothespian character of a smaller town, as Mrs Jordan was of Chester in 1809,[17] an engagement could be made upon a "certainty" rather than on shares, in which case no benefit was due. But even when this was the arrangement, the manager seldom desired to forego the adventitious attraction of the word "benefit" on his bills during a star's visit, and in memoirs we catch sight of some of these nominal benefits. When John Bernard and his wife were invited by Tate Wilkinson to play at York for six weeks in the summer, about 1770, 'he ensured us sixty guineas, he taking our benefits.'[18] On Bannister's visit to Dublin in 1796, the arrangement was more elaborate, as possible presents on the nominal benefit were taken into consideration.

> Bannister was at his own expense to go to Dublin, to play twelve nights at Daly's theatre and no other, three nights in a week, and to receive for each night fifty pounds. He was to play two additional nights without any salary, the one nominally for his own benefit the other avowedly for that of Daly; but all the money was to be the pérquisite of the manager unless it should happen that some friends of the performers might make gratuitous presents, or pay extra prices for tickets; in which case the surplus money, on his own night, was to remain with the performer.[19]

A case will be mentioned in its place later of the outside patron becoming guarantor of the benefit charges, but this concerned Mrs Charke, whose credit was so negligible that it always called for solid guarantees.

Hibernian theatricals were always highly individual, and in 1760 Tate Wilkinson's benefit at Smock-alley, Dublin, was so overwhelmingly successful that 'another night was demanded for the outstanding tickets,'[20] this overflow benefit taking place six days later with a gross of £150, against a nightly average of £40 at the time. This practice has not been noticed elsewhere, though we do find what is really its converse, as when at Swansea in 1811, two

[17] A. Aspinall, op. cit., pp. 112, 120.
[18] John Bernard, op. cit., I, 149.
[19] John Adolphus, op. cit., I, 380.
[20] Life of Mrs Abington, p. 23.

actors received a second benefit, 'because heat, illness and accident had kept many supporters from the first.'[21] Provincial managers knew how to be generous to keep a good company contented, and De Camp at Newcastle when, upon the death of King George III in 1820, the theatre was closed for a fortnight, reopened with a "Free Benefit" for the players.[22]

A type of benefit to which actors were sometimes subjected in smaller provincial companies, and which was objectionable to many of them, came to be known as "lumping", and consisted of a compulsory pooling of the benefits and their proceeds. The disadvantages of this are most clearly set out by the ever-aggrieved Everard.

> I could have no chance of a benefit at Reading, and we were compelled to go three in a benefit at Weybridge, or not take any. I had innocently said, that independently of my interest there, I could fill half the house by my Chertsey friends, a distance of only three short miles. This simple declaration caused a little envy and jealousy with some of the company, who could not bear the idea of my having a single benefit; and, small as the theatre was, clearing perhaps ten pounds, when they might not clear ten shillings. They therefore resolved to lump the benefits and all share and share alike.[23] *

At Norwich in the 1770's the custom was that in the city itself benefits were individual, but while playing on the surrounding circuit of East Anglian towns, the benefits were "lumped", unless any benefit, announced, of course, as that of a particular artist, grossed £30 or more, when it became individual.

Considering the still primitive nature of provincial theatricals in the first half of the 18th century before the following decades which saw the building of so many theatres out of London, the benefit arrangements were often of a remarkable complexity.

Some years ago Miss Sybil Rosenfeld discovered in a notebook in the Bristol Library some particulars of the accounts of the company playing at the Jacob's Well Theatre in Bristol from 1741 to 1748, which throw light upon provincial benefit customs in those early days. The nightly expenses were about £5 in the earlier and £8 in the later years of this period. Though the company was on the sharing system, benefits were taken, which ran up to a maximum of

---

[21] Cecil Price, *op. cit.*, p. 104.
[22] Harold Oswald, *op. cit.*, p. 68.
[23] E. C. Everard, *op. cit.*, p. 153.

£76. In general on benefit nights fixed shares of 5/- were distributed to the members of the company, but there seem to have been two other arrangements in operation at various times, one by which the beneficiary agreed to give the rest of the company a lump sum for their collective salaries for his benefit—£10 being one of the sums named—, the other by which a player would have a "half" benefit, sharing after expenses exclusive of salaries, not with the manager, but with the company as a whole.[24]

The provincial theatres and companies had their own equivalent of the metropolitan second benefit granted for special success or special services. This might be termed a post-seasonal benefit, and a few instances will make clear its nature. The player thus singled out could rely upon the theatre, scenery and wardrobe; his difficulty was to assemble a company. Everard, when he was playing at Weymouth at the end of the 18th century, and had taken his seasonal benefit, writes:

> In a week after we closed; and when the manager and I had settled all accounts and expences, he appeared so well satisfied with my exertions, that he made me a compliment of three guineas, in addition to the salary he had agreed to pay me; notwithstanding I had a good benefit, he also gave me the free use of the theatre, scenes and properties, gratis, for another night. I accordingly engaged a few of the performers, who could stay, by paying them their night's salaries, which with music, lights, and bills, making my expences very easy, I cleared nearly as much by this benefit . . . as I did by the first.[25]

There was not a great deal of difference at North Shields in 1842 when the manager favoured an actor named Gifford in this way. In this case the whole entertainments of the evening were provided by the beneficiary, his wife, son, and three daughters, and they are said to have presented 'an amusement free from immorality, calculated to blend instruction with innocent recreation.'[26]

In the lesser theatrical companies, which went on a circuit of theatres and barn-theatres in smaller country towns, with salaries varying from 15/- to 30/- per week, there is another quaint benefit phenomenon to be observed. When benefit time came round, the

[24] Sybil Rosenfeld, *Actors in Bristol 1741-8*, in *Times Literary Supplement*, August 29, 1936.
[25] E. C. Everard, *op. cit.*, p. 162.
[26] Robert King, *op. cit.*, p. 75.

end of the wretched hunger-pinched season was already in sight, and as these poor players dreaded the considerable fatigue of learning a number of new parts for the benefit of others, there was a tendency for each, when his or her own benefit had been taken, to slip away deserting the company, which would be left in the final week or two with only its basic family nucleus plus those players whose benefits had not yet come round.[27] The information about this nuance of the benefit system refers to the 1830's, but the difficulty would have been present, possibly in a still more exaggerated form, fifty years earlier.

Below is set out a short list of some provincial benefit charges noted at various times in different cities, with the addition of the capacity of the theatre where this is known to the writer.

City	Year	Charge	Capacity	Note
Bath	1809	£100		28
Birmingham	1804	£40	£250	29
Brighton	1778	£20		30
Bristol	1741	£5	£75	31
	1748	£8	£75	31
	1809	£100		32
Dublin	1783	£60		33
	1809	£52-10	£540	34
	1821	£80		35
Dundee	1834	£14		36
Edinburgh	1766	£25		37
	1780	£35	£100	38
	1817	£30		39
Guernsey	1792	£10		40
Liverpool	1821	£55-£60	£300	41
Swansea	1805	£8	£30	42
York	1740	£4		43

[27] "Peter Paterson", *Glimpses of Real Life, as seen in the Theatrical World and in Bohemia*, Edinburgh, 1864, p. 46.
[28] A. Aspinall, *op. cit.*, p. 82. [29] *Biographical Memoir of William West Betty*, London, 1805, p. 17. [30] E. C. Everard, *op. cit.*, p. 72. [31] Sybil Rosenfeld, *Actors in Bristol, 1741-8*, in *Times Literary Supplement*, August 29, 1936. [32] A. Aspinall, *op. cit.*, p. 82. [33] Charles Lee Lewes, *op. cit.*, I, 101. [34] Walter Donaldson, *op. cit.*, p. 48. [35] *History of the Theatre Royal, Dublin*, p. 45. [36] Peter Baxter, *op. cit.*, p. 216. [37] Charles Lee Lewes, *op. cit.*, III, 71. [38] Tate Wilkinson, *The Wandering Patentee*, II, 88. [39] E. C. Everard, *op. cit.*, p. 269. [40] John Bernard, *op. cit.*, II, 254. [41] *Liverpool Theatrical Investigator*, I, 58, 488. [42] E. C. Everard, *op. cit.*, p. 232. [43] Tate Wilkinson, *The Wandering Patentee*, II, 206.

VIII—CHARITY BENEFITS

STAGE FOLK HAVE ALWAYS SHOWN THEMSELVES so warm hearted and so willing to lavish their talents and energies for any deserving cause, that charity benefits are multifarious, but as the most enduring part of the benefit system, the main types should be distinguished.

Charity benefits, then, were of five kinds, those associated with public disasters or occasions when public sympathy was aroused; those for hospitals and general charitable objects; those of a patriotic nature; those for deserving individuals not associated with the theatre, a type of benefit confined to the 18th century; and those for members of the profession who had fallen upon sickness or hard times, and for dependents in the case of the sudden death of an artist.

Extensive fires called for immediate charitable relief in the 18th century when fire insurance was in its infancy. Benefits realizing £426 were given at Drury Lane and Covent Garden in 1748 for 'the poor sufferers from a remarkable and dreadful fire in Cornhill' (Quin returning from Bath to play at Covent Garden),[1] and at Drury Lane in 1760 'for the sufferers of the late fire in King Street.'[2]

In 1782 the public was deeply shocked by the accidental loss with all hands of Admiral Kempenfeldt's flagship the *Royal George* while careening, and a benefit given for the widows at Portsmouth realized £220.[3] A later naval disaster, the loss of the *Eurydice* in 1878, evoked a benefit at the Gaiety with what must have been the extraordinary sight of the portly and bewhiskered W. S. Gilbert disporting himself in the spangles of Harlequin after the pantomime of *The Forty Thieves*. *Punch* with awed respect described him as 'a very Titan among Harlequins.'[4]

At different times between 1820 and 1850 the distressed condition of both the Irish and Scottish peasants aroused sufficient concern to be considered in the category of public disasters. The Irish suffered

[1] Tate Wilkinson, *Memoirs of His Own Life*, III, 186, and Charles B. Hogan, *Shakespeare in the Theatre 1701-1750*, Oxford, 1952, p. 78.

[2] Percy Fitzgerald, *Life of David Garrick*, II, 478.

[3] E. C. Everard, *op. cit.*, p. 35.

[4] Clement Scott and Cecil Howard, *op. cit.*, II, 476, and note, and Leslie Bailey, *The Gilbert and Sullivan Book*, London, 1952, p. 139.

especially in the hard winter of 1822, and their distresses found sympathy, especially in Scotland where charity benefits were given in Dundee, Arbroath and Perth. At the latter city the particular became engagingly intermingled with the general, for a part of the proceeds of the benefit was applied 'to defray the expenses of a meritorious but unfortunate actress on her journey to Ireland, her native country.'[5]

About the earlier of these two dates some of the more far-seeing stars conceived the idea of subordinating present profit to the attainment of the enduring good-will of the inhabitants of important adjacent capitals such as Dublin. So we find Edmund Kean in the same year of 1822 devoting the proceeds of his Drury Lane benefit to the 'Relief of the Distressed Peasantry in the Sister Kingdom.' But alas by 1822 Kean was on the downward path, having just returned in disgrace from America, and the distressed peasantry only benefited to the tune of just over £5.[6]

At one time, between about 1830 and 1860, the public benefit fell somewhat into disrepute, as it became in fact little more than an excuse for stage-struck amateurs to exhibit themselves. At one such performance at the St James's in 1847 in the presence of the Queen 'for the benefit of the distressed peasantry of Scotland and Ireland,' a dramatist who had a piece in the bill was at the stage door when a leading member of the amateur company arrived, and greeted him with the ominous words 'My dear Planché, I am very drunk.'[7]

More honourable public benefits by amateurs were the "joint stock" extravaganzas, written, composed and played by members of the Savage Club at the Lyceum in the early 1860's, one of which, attended by the Queen, Prince Consort and Prince of Wales, and afterwards repeated in Liverpool, was in aid of the Lancashire cotton operatives rendered unemployed by the American Civil War.[8]

A public disaster associated with the theatre itself made special claims. As a result of a false alarm of fire at Sadler's Wells in 1807, eighteen people were killed on the gallery stairs, and the management gave three benefits for the dependants of the victims.[9]

Hospitals, if they were inadequately endowed, ranked high among deserving objects for general charitable assistance from the theatres,

[5] Peter Baxter, op. cit., pp. 117, 118.
[6] H. N. Hillebrand, op. cit., p. 226.
[7] J. R. Planché, Recollections and Reflections, London, 1872, II, 140, 141.
[8] Ibid., II, 215, and Clement Scott and Cecil Howard, op. cit., I, 183 note.
[9] Thomas Dibdin, op. cit., I, 404.

and Garrick gave benefits at Drury Lane for the Lock Hospital in 1747 and 1755.[10] But even hospital benefits did not always surmount the less agreeable aspects of human nature, and some half a century later Mrs Siddons, on her visit to Dublin in 1802, was unfortunate enough to run into a squabble over an allegation that she had refused to play at a benefit for the Lying-in Hospital. The truth seems to be that she promised Jones the Dublin manager to play for *a* public charity during her visit, the object to be selected by Lady Hardwicke the Vicereine, and it was generally assumed that the Lying-in Hospital would be selected. Jones, for his own reasons, did not follow up her offer, but she was blamed.[11]

Those imprisoned for debt were assured of the ready sympathy of the players, who, as will be shown in the last chapter of this book, were themselves unusually vulnerable to such a fate. Garrick gave a benefit for the Marshalsea Prisoners at Drury Lane in 1750,[12] and when in 1793 a benefit was given at Newcastle for 'the poor debtors confined in Newgate', the matter had been thought out, and the play-bill explained that it was not proposed to divide the profits of the night in equal proportions among the prisoners, but 'to liberate some one debtor, who may be found upon enquiry a real object of charity.'[13] There is just a foreshadowing hint here of the Victorian linking of relief with enquiry and deserts.

Following the example set by Kean in 1822, stars in the middle of the 19th century quite often nominated their own favourite objects of benevolence when appearing at charity benefits. Thus Rachel's last appearance at Drury Lane in 1855 under the patronage of Queen Victoria was for the benefit of the French Charitable Association.[14]

Nor were provincial theatres at all behindhand in such general works of charity. Among the deserving objects helped by benefit performances at various times were a baker who had lost his business through fire (Birmingham 1744),[15] the debt of the Blue Coat School (Birmingham c 1807),[16] and local hospitals at many different

[10] Percy Fitzgerald, *Life of David Garrick*, II, 476, and Charles B. Hogan, *op. cit.*, p. 76.

[11] James Boaden, *Life of Mrs Siddons*, II, 338.

[12] Percy Fitzgerald, *Life of David Garrick*, II, 473.

[13] Harold Oswald, *op. cit.*, p. 49.

[14] Edward Stirling, *Old Drury Lane*, London, 1881, I, 255.

[15] J. E. Cunningham, *op. cit.*, p. 13.

[16] *Ibid.*, p. 26.

places and times. The hospital benefit at Birmingham in 1887 was a particularly imposing affair of three consecutive performances, two by amateurs and one by the Benson company, to celebrate the jubilee of the manager of the Theatre Royal.[17] Brighton came to the aid of the Italian and Spanish refugees (1827),[18] and, rather nearer home, the survivors of the packet *Nancy* (1818).[19] Against these provincial public benefits may be set the awkward incident at Exeter in the 1870's when 'the Committee of the Devon and Exeter Hospital, at the instance of a clergyman, declined to accept the offer of the proceeds of a performance at the theatre.'[20]

The "Poor" in the wider sense were, from the nature of the problem their relief presented, more a local or provincial than a general metropolitan responsibility. Yet in their own districts the minor theatres of London joined in to the best of their ability, and in 1816, which was a very hard winter, when 'the poor were hourly crying out for food,' Tom Dibdin, then managing the Surrey Theatre, wrote 'in one week I gave six charity benefits, which I grieve to say were very indifferently attended.'[21]

During the 19th century benefits were not infrequently given for the widespread network of local Philanthropic Societies then existing in London, some of which survive. For instance the Euston Philanthropic Society received a benefit at the Haymarket on November 26, 1863 'to enable the Committee to distribute liberally to the Poor — Meat, Bread, Groceries, and Coals, the ensuing Christmas.'[22]

In the provinces, starting quite early in the 18th century, charity benefits came to be a recognized means of conciliating the magistrates or otherwise obtaining the goodwill of the authorities. 'Where a circuit was established, a play for the benefit of the poor of each town or the prisoners in the gaols, came to be expected.'[23] Such an occasion as the inauguration of a new theatre would call for a charity benefit; for instance on the opening of the new Theatre Royal, Norwich in 1826 (a building which survived fire until 1934),

[17] E. L. Levy, *Birmingham Theatrical Reminiscences*, Birmingham, n.d. [c. 1905], pp. 20-22.
[18] H. C. Porter, *op. cit.*, pp. 55, 56.
[19] *Ibid.*, p. 47.
[20] William Cotton, *The Story of the Drama in Exeter*, Exeter, 1887, p. 11.
[21] Thomas Dibdin, *op. cit.*, II, 133.
[22] Playbill in the Author's collection.
[23] Cecil Price, *op. cit.*, p. 12.

the proceeds of the first night, £120, were applied to the fund for the distressed poor, 'that season unfortunately very numerous in the city.'[24]

But this custom of a performance, usually the opening one of a new season, being given for the local poor, did not pass unquestioned in puritanical Scotland. In May 1817 when Corbett Ryder made his announcement of this proposed benefit at Perth, an anonymous correspondent in the local press retorted that the action of Mr Ryder and his company of actors in giving the first night as a benefit night was because they expected to receive twenty times as much in return; took exception to people going to theatres when so much distress existed, and added that people who had spare cash might give it to the fund and forego going to the theatre.[25]

Patriotic benefits began quite early, one at the Haymarket in 1744 being for 'a brave soldier that suffered extremely at the battle of Dettingen.'[26] The benefits in 1746 for what was called the "Veteran's Fund", for the recompense of Volunteers who had turned out against the Rebellion of 1745, occasioned some squabbling and heartburning. Mrs Cibber was the leading spirit, and when Lacy proved obstructive over lending Drury Lane, she accepted Rich's offer of Covent Garden.[27] There was great public enthusiasm, and even 'the tallow chandlers gave the candles.'[28] Three performances were given, with Mrs Cibber playing three different characters on the successive nights, the amount raised being £602.[29]

At the outset of the Napoleonic wars, the military side of patriotic benevolence often took a strictly practical turn, and in Newcastle in November 1793 the profits of a benefit were 'to purchase flannel waistcoats, shoes, socks, caps etc for the better clothing of our brave countrymen who are fighting our battles under the command of His Highness the Duke of York at this inclement season.'[30] But the recipient's appreciation of flannel waistcoats varied with the distance from the firing line, and what may have been appreciated on the island of Walcheren at an inclement season did not preclude a display of temperament by Volunteers in Devon. During the season

[24] Bosworth Harcourt, *op. cit.*, p. 6.
[25] Peter Baxter, *op. cit.*, p. 43.
[26] Charles B. Hogan, *op. cit.*, p. 68.
[27] *The Private Correspondence of David Garrick*, I, 45, 46.
[28] William Dunlap, *op. cit.*, I, 223.
[29] John Fyvie, *op. cit.*, p. 84.
[30] Harold Oswald, *op. cit.*, pp. 49, 50.

1803-1804, when the bogey of invasion had not yet been laid by the guns of Trafalgar, *Henry V* was given at Exeter, 'and it was intended that the whole receipts of the night should be applied in aid of the ladies fund for supplying the Exeter Volunteers with flannel waistcoats, but some of the privates thought it derogatory to their character and consequence to accept of them, so the offer was declined.'[31]

The remaining wars of the 19th century brought the same benefit pattern. The Crimea came in the heyday of the big benefit by fashionable amateurs, and in this war benevolence was consolidated in the Crimean Army Fund, the full title of which was 'the Fund now raising by Royal Commission for the Widows and Orphans of the brave men who have fallen in the Crimea.'[32]

At the outbreak of the South African War, Mrs Beerbohm Tree recited Kipling's *Absent-Minded Beggar* at the Palace Theatre, then a music-hall, for ten weeks; her salary she gave to war charities, and the audience also showered gold and silver onto the stage.[33]

The British Tar never failed to arouse the enthusiastic support of the playgoing public, and the manifestations of this were varied. What was probably the first such occasion was the performance of *The Tempest* at Drury Lane on November 28, 1740 for the benefit of,

> the brave and unfortunate crew of the *Prince of Orange*, belonging to Capt. Peddie, who (after having clear'd themselves by the most gallant behaviour from a Spanish privateer) were shipwreck'd in a tempest in Margate Road, and stood on the wreck upward of twelve hours, with the sea beating over them, before they were relieved.[34]

The series of naval victories during the Napoleonic wars excited compassion for the dependents of the fallen. Public benefits were given at Drury Lane and Covent Garden respectively for the widows and orphans of the seamen who fell in the battles of the Glorious First of June in 1794, and Cape St Vincent in 1797. Duncan's victory off the Dutch coast in the latter year was similarly treated.[35] At the

[31] William Cotton, *op. cit.*, p. 19.

[32] Clement Scott and Cecil Howard, *op. cit.*, I, 129, and note 2 and Robert King, *op. cit.*, p. 89.

[33] Max Beerbohm and others, *Herbert Beerbohm Tree*, London, n.d. [c. 1920], pp. 112, 113.

[34] Charles B. Hogan, *op. cit.*, p. 56.

[35] James Boaden, *Life of Mrs Jordan*, Vol. I, p. 345.

first benefit the piece produced 'concluded with an awfully grand sea fight'[36] when 'the spectators coughed and enjoyed the powder.'[37] At the latter Mrs Abington emerged after seven years of retirement to speak the Epilogue.[38]

Of benefits for more general patriotic objects during the Napoleonic wars, first mention is earned by the anticipatory foresight of that at Newcastle in May 1793 for 'the widows and children of the seamen and soldiers who may die or be killed in His Majesty's Service during the present war.'[39] Still more general was the night given at Covent Garden in January 1798 'for the voluntary contribution for the defence of our country'[40] and it may be wondered quite how the profits were allocated. Lloyds Patriotic Fund, which in addition to the usual distribution of money, also presented swords of honour to individual officers who had distinguished themselves, was a popular collective outlet for patriotic feelings, and received £537 from the receipts of the opening night at Drury Lane in the season 1803-1804.[41] In 1812 Drury Lane gave a benefit for 'the British prisoners of war in France.'[42]

Benefits in the 18th century for deserving individuals with slight or no apparent theatrical connection were not infrequent. Misfortune, distress, trouble and necessity are the four sad keywords of this type of philanthropic non-theatrical benefit in the first half of the 18th century. The five theatres of Drury Lane, Covent Garden, Lincoln's Inn Fields, the Haymarket and Goodman's Fields were equally assiduous in providing relief. One single source consulted by the writer lists thirty-nine such casual beneficiaries, sometimes named, more often anonymous. The most representative figure is 'a gentleman under misfortune'; there are five of his ilk between 1723 and 1747, while quite astonishingly in 1734 one of them shared a benefit at Covent Garden with two named actors of the company, Aston and Thompson.[43]

A selection of recipients will give the flavour of this kind of benevolence:

[36] M. J. Young, *Memoirs of Mrs Crouch*, London, 1806, II, 217.
[37] James Boaden, *Life of Mrs Jordan*, I, 266.
[38] *Life of Mrs Abington*, p. 100.
[39] Harold Oswald, *op. cit.*, p. 49.
[40] M. J. Young, *op. cit.*, II, 288.
[41] James Boaden, *Life of Mrs Jordan*, I, 136.
[42] Thomas Dibdin, *op. cit.*, II, 9.
[43] Charles B. Hogan, *op. cit.*, p. 44.

a poor distress'd citizen's widow, and six children . . . a gentleman who has wrote for the stage . . . a young gentlewoman,
distress'd by the bankruptcy of her guardian . . . an unfortunate brother Mason . . . a gentleman reduc'd by the late
general misfortune [i.e. the South Sea Bubble] . . . an antient
widow gentlewoman . . . a person who has been a great sufferer
in trade, and is now under confinement for debt.[44]

One is entitled to wonder just how these unfortunate and distress'd
persons were selected from the mass of their kind, and how the
managements obtained the willing co-operation of the actors to
such haphazard charity.

In 1750 Garrick gave a performance of *Comus* for Milton's aged
granddaughter and raised £130.[45] Dr Johnson twice used his
influence to obtain theatrical benefits for Mrs Anna Williams, a
blind authoress and translator, who was a protegée of his.

There were also some curious benefit affairs in the 18th century
of an indeterminate nature, in which an amateur cast was stiffened
by two or three lesser professionals. Here is the opening of the
account of such a one about 1765:

A family in distress had applied to the Lord Chamberlain for
his permission, and to Mr Foot, the manager of the theatre in
the Haymarket, for a benefit play, in which they succeeded, but
were under the utmost dejection for want of a hero, to perform
the principal character.[46]

What must have been one of the last of such benefits, poised as it
were between the theatrical and the non-theatrical, took place at the
Haymarket in February 1801, out of the normal summer season of
that theatre, when, 'Under the Patronage of His Royal Highness the
Duke of Cumberland And by permission of the Lord Chamberlain,
For the benefit of Lady Perrott and her Orphan Family, the settlement of whose Affairs being unfortunately protracted', *The Earl of
Essex* was played with the beneficiary in the role of Queen Elizabeth.[47] The nature of her ladyship's protracted Affairs and her
qualifications for playing a leading part both excite curiosity.

In the 19th century the benefit for non-theatrical individuals dies
away. One interesting exception was in 1867 when a lesser member

[44] *Ibid.*, pp. 24, 25, 34, 61, 71, 80, 83.
[45] Percy Fitzgerald, *Life of David Garrick*, II, 473.
[46] Thomas Snagg, *op. cit.*, p. 26.
[47] Playbill in Garrick Club Collection.

of *Punch* staff named Bennett died, and the staff 'got up a first-rate benefit for him'—or more properly for his dependents. These beneficiaries were fortunate in that at the time many of the leading members of the staff of the paper were dramatists and burlesque writers in the closest touch with the stage. *Cox and Box,* by Burnand and Sullivan, adapted from Maddison Morton's old farce, and still well-known from its place in the D'Oyly Carte repertoire, was played for the first time, and a second benefit for the same object was also given at Manchester, the provincial première of *Cox and Box.*[48]

Where benefits for professionals in misfortune were concerned, there is one quite early instance of a play being performed by amateurs. Mrs Becky Wells, always in trouble, was lent the Haymarket for a night (presumably out of season), on condition that she secured a guarantor for the charges, which she achieved, and 'all the male dramatis personae were gentlemen of independent fortune.'[49]

Earlier still Mrs Charke, another lady always in trouble, is last heard of, also at the Haymarket, as a beneficiary in 1759, the year before her death, her appeal running, 'As I am entirely dependent upon chance for a subsistence and desirous of settling into business. I humbly trust the town will favour me on the occasion.'[50]

What might be termed collective benefits to meet theatrical distress were frequently on a large scale and always well supported. When Drury Lane was burned down in 1809, the company moved to the Opera House and announced three nights 'for their common benefit', with the assistance of the Opera ballet. The receipt of the first was £549, and of the third, when Mrs Jordan played, £834. This public support was so encouraging that three more nights were announced. Madame Catalini sang to a house of £903, and the six performances grossed £4,266. As a result the principal performers received 75% of their salaries, the second class 87½%, and the third class their full demands.[51]

On the humble level of the lesser "minors", the disaster of fire, the ever-present menace to all of them, made for an instant general rallying round the sufferer. When the Garrick, in Leman Street, Whitechapel, was burnt down in 1846, the other East End theatres,

[48] Francis C. Burnand, *Records and Reminiscences,* London, 1904, II, 233.
[49] *Life of Mrs Sumbel, late Wells,* II, 147, 148.
[50] *A Narrative of the Life of Mrs Charlotte Charke,* p. 9.
[51] George Raymond, *op. cit.,* p. 154.

the City of London, the Standard, the Pavilion, the Britannia and the Effingham, had one and all offered their theatres for benefit performances within three days.[52]

The Surrey Theatre was rather more important, and when in 1865 it too was burnt down, a benefit performance with many stars was given at Drury Lane for the Surrey company within a fortnight, the bill including an act of *Black-eyed Susan,* the most famous piece ever produced at the Surrey. This is a nice instance of a senior theatre giving prompt help to the company of a distinguished "minor" when in affliction.[53]

But this kind of support for metropolitan happenings did not extend beyond London itself. When in 1828 Brighton intervened in such a case with a benefit, 'The fund to relieve the sufferers through the fall of the Brunswick Theatre (in the East End of London), though patronised by the Hon Mrs Ongly . . . amounted to only £28-10.'[54] The provincial theatres accepted, however, their own collective obligations, and when the Bath manager left his company in the lurch after the disastrous season of 1841-1842 there, a committee of local citizens organized two benefit performances.[55] A benefit was similarly organized at Brighton, with the band of the 4th Dragoons, when the manager departed in a hurry in 1854.[56]

The big benefits for the sick or aged player come in sad procession down the decades — Mrs Saunders, 'many years a comedian', had one at Covent Garden in 1744[57] — though by the 1760's both the Patent Theatres had their Theatrical Funds, which amounted to £60,000 on their amalgamation in the 19th century. Garrick devoted the proceeds of his final performance to the Drury Lane Fund.[58] The only known refusal to play for the Fund was that (through his father) of Master Betty, the Young Roscius, during his extraordinary vogue in 1805.[59] When later these Funds had become the Royal General Theatrical Fund, annual all-star benefits were given, and, quite in the modern spirit, E. A. Sothern, although then playing in

[52] Frances Fleetwood, *Conquest,* London, 1953, p. 53.
[53] Clement Scott and Cecil Howard, *op. cit.,* I, 306 and note.
[54] H. C. Porter, *op. cit.,* p. 57.
[55] S. Penley, *op. cit.,* pp. 141, 142.
[56] H. C. Porter, *op. cit.,* pp. 95, 96.
[57] Charles B. Hogan, *op. cit.,* p. 67.
[58] Percy Fitzgerald, *Life of David Garrick,* II, 167.
[59] James Boaden, *Life of Mrs Jordan,* I, 188.

America, crossed the Atlantic both ways in order to appear at that in 1872.[60]

In addition to various consolidated charitable Funds of the profession, an institution was founded in the middle of the 19th century with the confusing name of the Dramatic College. This was in no sense a Conservatoire or early Royal Academy of Dramatic Art: it was a polite term for a sort of super almshouse for aged actors and actresses. The Council of this College shocked many worthy people in the 1860's, but raised a good deal of money, by a now forgotten anticipation of the later Theatrical Garden Party (for the Actors' Orphanage), which was a feature of the London season for many years and only terminated in 1953 for such economic reasons as the increasing cost of hire of marquees, etc. The Dramatic College gambols took place in the grounds of the Crystal Palace in the form of an old-fashioned Fair, with many leading players prepared nearly 100 years ago to take part in undignified fairground antics for a theatrical charity. In 1861 this Dramatic College received a benefit at the Italian Opera which lasted 5½ hours from 7 p.m. to 1.35 a.m., with scenes from seven different pieces played, and almost every actor and actress of note taking part.[61]

Mrs Bellamy, six years after her retirement, was given a big charity benefit at Covent Garden in 1785, on which occasion Mrs Yates emerged from semi-retirement to play for her.[62] When the curtain went up to discover her seated on a chair on the stage, the whole house rose. She tried to rise too, but could not, though finally she muttered a few words expressive of her gratitude.[63] Charles Bannister, immensely popular and with the advantage of a son active in the theatre, managed after his retirement to obtain an annual benefit at the Haymarket, that in 1800 being attended by Lord Nelson with Sir William and Lady Hamilton, all just returned from the Mediterranean.[64] The dependents of John Emery, portrayer of rustic characters and ancestor of Winifred Emery (Mrs Cyril Maude) had a great benefit at Drury Lane in 1822, which realized £948.[65]

[60] T. Edgar Pemberton, op. cit., p. 109.
[61] Clement Scott and Cecil Howard, op. cit., I, 256 and note 2.
[62] John Fyvie, op. cit., p. 143.
[63] Frederick Reynolds, op. cit., I, 282.
[64] John Adolphus, op. cit., II, 66.
[65] Memoirs of J. S. Munden, p. 47, and H. C. Porter, op. cit., p. 50.

Grimaldi, greatest of Clowns, worn out at the age of fifty, was given a benefit in 1828 that raised £580.

Widows, orphans and dependents were provided for with almost unfailing regularity, and where the case seemed to call for promptitude, this was forthcoming. When Mr Inchbald died at York on June 7, 1779 'the Widow Inchbald's benefit was on Monday, June 14, 1779, and very genteelly attended.'[66] The widow of Charles Macklin, the actor who had died in 1797 at the age of 97 and possibly more, was given a benefit bringing in about £300 at Covent Garden in 1805, for which Kemble, Cooke and Mrs Jordan played.[67] Dramatists' widows or relations had their benefits too, and a most unusual such benefit enterprise took place at Covent Garden in 1749. James Thomson, author of a tragedy *Coriolanus,* had died the previous autumn leaving a sister destitute, and either she or her brother seems to have been a favourite of the company, as five benefit performances of his play were given for her, four of them consecutive.[68] The circumstances must have been very exceptional for managerial sanction to be obtained for such wholesale benevolence, and during the entire 200-year period there are less than half a dozen instances of more than one consecutive benefit for the same object .

The widow of Haynes Bayly the dramatist was helped with a benefit in 1839. 'She shrank at first from the publicity of such an appeal, but at length consented.'[69] This benefit had the unusual feature that two of the late dramatist's own pieces were performed, one played by the Haymarket company, the other by the Olympic company. The widow and children of Elton, the actor drowned at sea in 1843, were also given a big benefit, for which Hood wrote a poem,[70] though a similar benefit for them at Brighton only raised £40.[71]

Fanny Kelly, a favourite at Drury Lane since 1800, who had lost her fortune trying to establish a school of acting at the Royalty, was given in 1846 a benefit by "The Amateurs", who included Dickens, Mark Lemon, Douglas Jerrold, Leech, Forster and George Cruickshank. Seven years later a still larger benefit for her in the presence of Queen Victoria was planned, but had to be abandoned owing to

---

[66] Tate Wilkinson, *The Wandering Patentee,* II, 64.
[67] James Boaden, *Life of Mrs Jordan,* I, 191.
[68] Janet Camden Lucey, *op. cit.,* p. 142, and John Genest, *op. cit.,* IV, 279.
[69] J. R. Planché, *op. cit.,* II, 11-13, and Alfred Bunn, *op. cit.,* III, 212, 213.
[70] J. R. Planché, *op. cit.,* I, 100.
[71] H. C. Porter, *op. cit.,* p. 79.

Fanny Kelly's illness and that of Dickens, who was the organizer.[72]

Douglas Jerrold, who died in 1857, was in a particularly favoured position, since he had been a dramatist for thirty years, a prolific journalist and editor of *Punch*. In consequence a whole series of benefit entertainments was given for his widow and family that is probably without parallel. There were two full theatrical benefit nights of performances of his plays, one at the Haymarket of *The Housekeeper* and *The Prisoner of War* with two members of the original casts, and one at the Adelphi of *The Rent Day* and *Black-eyed Susan*. There were also a concert at St Martin's Hall, readings by Charles Dickens, an account of his Crimean doings by W. H. Russell (the *Times* correspondent), and an entertainment by a literary amateur troupe at the Gallery of Illustration, a small theatre in Lower Regent Street so called in order to bamboozle the consciences of those Victorians who could not bear to set foot in a theatre.[73]

Another example of the combined amateur and professional benefit, and a very notable one, was that for the widow of Charles Calvert, who had produced eleven Shakespeare plays in Manchester, all but one at the Prince's Theatre, between 1864 and 1874. The play was *As You Like It*; Miss Helen Faucit was drawn from her retirement to play Rosalind, and the rest of the company consisted of a combination of the amateur talent on the staff of *Punch* (George du Maurier and Linley Sambourne), two well-known dramatists (Tom Taylor and Herman Merivale) and the cream of the Manchester amateur talent.

The relief of sickness during the player's working life spans the whole benefit period. In 1722 'Chr. Bullock, who in great distress, has kept his chamber these two months, under a severe and expensive sickness' received £117 from a benefit at Lincoln's Inn Fields.[74] In the second half of the 19th century the benefit custom still sometimes included the gracious provision of a fresh financial start for an artist long absent through illness. For instance, in 1887 an esteemed actress Miss Phillips, who had suffered a long and serious illness, enjoyed a Haymarket benefit with a dozen front-rank stars playing, and afterwards returned to the stage in 1890.[75] Rather

[72] Basil Francis, *Fanny Kelly of Drury Lane*, London, 1950, pp. 182, 187.
[73] Clement Scott and Cecil Howard, *op. cit.*, I, 177 and note 1.
[74] Charles B. Hogan, *op. cit.*, p. 24.
[75] E. Reid and H. Compton, *The Dramatic Peerage 1892*, London, 1892, p. 170.

similarly at Birmingham a deserving actress of the former stock company, Miss Burchell, was given a benefit by the united amateur talent of the city in 1890, long after the stock company had ceased to exist.[76]

Of later individual benefits the two of which the echoes lingered longest were the public's farewell at Drury Lane to two very diverse favourites, both greatly beloved, Nellie Farren in 1898 and Ellen Terry upon her jubilee in 1906, the sums raised being £5,000 and £6,000. In both cases we read of an enormous programme with every star in London appearing, of the beneficiary sitting with her family around her, Nellie Farren in black, Ellen Terry in white, of wild cheering and the singing of "Old Lang Syne". Nellie Farren was an invalid, and could only say 'Thank ye, sir', a line from her famous street-Arab song, while Ellen Terry made quite a long speech, and actually did not make her last appearance on the stage until fourteen years later.[77]

The modern variant takes the form of a "midnight matinée" at which all stars are available to appear after their own shows. These performances might be called "endowment benefits", for, as the incidence of present day taxation precludes individual provision for dependents by even the thrifty, the final tribute of the profession itself must be invoked for the endowment of children's proper education and the like. In 1951 a popular comedian Sid Field, whose rise had been rapid, died suddenly, and the considerable sum of £15,000 was raised for his children at a midnight matinée. It is safe to prophesy that this form of charity benefit will increase.

In addition to the definitely charitable benefit, theatre history shows also quite a range of benefits, mostly in the provinces, in aid of objects or institutions deserving of popular support, and in just a few cases for objects that the theatrical profession itself had at heart.

Of benefits for these latter objects quite the most endearing was the performance of *Julius Caesar* at the Queen's Theatre in January 1707 for 'the encouragement of the comedians acting in the Hay-Market, and to enable them to keep the diversion of plays under a separate interest from operas.'[78]

[76] E. L. Levy, *op. cit.*, p. 8.
[77] James Agate, *Those Were the Nights*, London, n.d. [c. 1935], pp. 78-82, 143-145, quoting contemporary newspapers.
[78] Charles B. Hogan, *op. cit.*, p. 5.

The name of Shakespeare never failed to command the allegiance of the players. The monument to the memory of the poet in Westminster Abbey was erected by means of a fund to which benefit performances of two of his plays at Drury Lane in 1738 and Covent Garden in 1739 contributed £170 and £82 respectively.[79] The Birthplace itself was not neglected, and in 1746 the strolling company of John Ward, grandfather of Mrs Siddons and the other Kembles, devoted the proceeds of a performance of *Othello* at Stratford to the repair of Shakespeare's monument in the parish church.[80] Even the editor of Shakespeare', by which is meant Theobald, whose edition had been published in the previous year, received the compliment of a benefit at Drury Lane in 1734.[81] The tradition persisted down the years in theatres great and small: on the Tercentenary of Shakespeare's birth in 1864 the benefit performance at North Shields was to provide a Shakespeare section in the Mechanic's Institute Library.[82]

When the institution to be benefited had no theatrical aspect, the diversity of managerial benevolence was so wide that it can only be indicated by a few examples. At Drury Lane in 1706 *Hamlet* was played to benefit 'the charge of repairing and fitting up the chapel in Russel-Court.'[83] In 1769 a benefit performance was given at Sunderland for 'those Sons of Liberty, the Brave Corsicans,'[84] that being the year in which Boswell postured in Corsican costume at Garrick's Jubilee at Stratford, and the Brave Corsicans were more fashionable than they were to become in another thirty years or so. Finally there is the benefit performance of *Grandfather Whitehead* at Brighton in 1852 'for the benefit of the cricket club.'[85] This was indeed to give each side an innings in turn, for it has been seen that cricket clubs more prosperous than that of Brighton were frequent givers of "bespeaks" to the players.

Benefits of this nature led on to the rise in the 1880's of the late Victorian and Edwardian charity matinée for a "deserving cause". Emigration was held to be one of these deserving causes and the Colonial Emigration Society was a pioneer in this form of appeal. In

[79] *Ibid.*, p. 52. Drury Lane played *Julius Caesar*, Covent Garden *Hamlet*.
[80] Cecil Price, *op. cit.*, p. 39.
[81] Charles B. Hogan, *op. cit.*, p. 43.
[82] Robert King, *op. cit.*, p. 96.
[83] Charles B. Hogan, *op. cit.*, p. 4.
[84] Robert King, *op. cit.*, p. 17.
[85] H. C. Porter, *op. cit.*, p. 92.

1884 the Society raised £300 by a benefit under royal patronage at the Lyceum, and the next year at the Court gave the unusual programme of a comedy played by professionals followed by a new one-act comic opera played by amateurs.[86]

Finally mention should be made of at least one case in the theatre in which Charity was a legal subterfuge to cover the doubtful legality of a particular performance. When in June 1787 Palmer opened the Royalty Theatre in Wellclose Square in the East End of London, in defiance of the monopoly rights of the two Patent Theatres and relying mistakenly upon the supposed authority of the Constable of the Tower and the Tower Hamlets magistrates to grant a licence, the proceeds of the first night were dedicated to the London Hospital, so that the strength of the opposition could be tested without Palmer actually having committed an offence by being deemed to have acted 'for hire, gain, or reward.'[87] This subterfuge was unavailing, and the theatre was soon closed by the Lord Chamberlain.

[86] Clement Scott and Cecil Howard, *op. cit.*, II, 565, 573.
[87] John Adolphus, *op. cit.*, I, 156.

IX—THE DECLINE

THE ENDING OF THE BENEFIT SYSTEM is claimed for America by Lester Wallack,[1] who, at Wallack's Theatre, presumably in the 1870's, obtained the consent of his company to the maximum they had received for a benefit, while under his management, being tacked on to and spread over their weekly salaries in lieu.

Actually the decline of the system was a much more gradual affair and some of the progressive steps of the declension have already been noted in earlier pages. The first undermining came in the last two decades of the 18th century when the "nominal" benefit arose in the course of the dickerings and alternatives surrounding the terms of a star visit to a provincial theatre. Alfred Bunn, who had learned the business of theatre management in the provinces, imported this principle to London when, in the period 1830-1840 as manager of both Drury Lane and Covent Garden, he found himself in need of some economic protection against the grasping foreign singers and dancers whose importation was forced upon him by the demands of his audiences.

Meanwhile in 1821 Macready, always anxious to appear a gentleman rather than an actor, had refused to accept the presents of money, or "guineas", that had been considered inseparable from a benefit, lest he should feel embarrassed if subsequently at a dinnertable with the donor. This priggish gesture by one who some ten years later became the leader of the Stage, had its effect in taking much of the old warmth out of the benefit night. His attitude must have accelerated the arrival of the position taken up by the Keeleys, who played together in London from 1829 to 1869, though they were not snobs like Macready, and their standpoint is rather a curious one for their times.

I never had a benefit in London in the whole course of my professional engagements here. Nor did Mr Keeley. Once Macready proposed to my husband that we should take one at Drury Lane. But Mr Keeley always disapproved of such things, and said that if the public wanted to see us they ought to pay

[1] Lester Wallack, *op. cit.*, pp. 54, 55. *The Oxford Companion to the Theatre* (s.v. Benefit) gives this date as 1867-1868.

in the usual way, and not be asked to purchase tickets specially. So no special announcements were issued and the tickets were sold in the ordinary manner.[2]

Though these two instances are of an attitude that was in effect the disparagement of the benefit, there arose in the period 1830-1850 an opposite but equally destructive tendency, that of pushing the use of the benefit to lengths absurdly remote from the old conception of a personal reward to a player after the arduous and versatile work of a ten months season. When the tenancy of Covent Garden by Madame Vestris and Charles Mathews the younger (1840-1842) was ending in disaster with bankruptcy impending, the final performance was announced as Madame's benefit.[3] This sort of thing was either clearly ridiculous, or a paltry device to get another £100 into the house.

Very little less of an abuse of the established system was the practice instituted at the Princess's Theatre in 1853 by Mr and Mrs Charles Kean when they took their annual benefit on the first night of the production of Lord Byron's tragedy of *Sardanapalus,* which ran for sixty-one performances that season and thirty-two more on reopening the next season. They repeated this gambit in 1854 with *The Courier of Lyons,* in 1858 with *The Merchant of Venice* and in 1859 with *Henry V.* As Charles Kean was his own manager and backer by 1853, a benefit on a first night was nothing but a trick.[4]

But the true cause of the collapse of the benefit system came with the introduction of the "long run", principally by Dion Boucicault, in the 1860's. When the basis of an actor's engagement became the "run of the piece" rather than the season of about ten months, with the prospect of playing the same part one or two hundred nights in succession, there was introduced into theatrical affairs the element of financial stability that permitted of reasonable salaries being paid.

The old system and the new had already had one brief encounter as early as 1829, when at the Surrey Theatre Douglas Jerrold's nautical play *Black-eyed Susan* achieved the then quite astonishing total of over 400 performances. T. P. Cooke the leading man was

[2] Walter Goodmer, *The Keeleys, On the Stage and At Home,* London, 1895, pp. 91, 92.

[3] Charles E. Pearce, *Madame Vestris and Her Times,* London, n.d., [c. 1908], p. 201.

[4] John Cole, *op. cit.,* II, 56, 57, 107, 262, and Clement Scott and Cecil Howard, *op. cit.,* I, 218 and note 3.

receiving £60 per week salary, and the ad hoc benefit arrangement made with him was that he should have 'half a clear benefit in every sixth week of representation.'[5]

The benefit lingered on at those theatres where a stock company was still in operation, such as the Haymarket, and in the provinces until the general rise of the touring company, but it was doomed. Sir Henry Irving, whose first appearance had been in 1856, kept the benefit going until 1891 and even beyond the line between sentiment and sense. After the year 1878 when he undertook the management of the Lyceum and was also his own backer, the taking of a benefit by him merely involved the transfer of a sum of money from one pocket to another, yet the ridiculous custom that he had learnt from Charles Kean was kept up with solemnity until 1887. Ellen Terry also took an annual benefit until 1895, though in her case it may well have represented a proper additional bonus to a salary remaining constant in face of increasing attraction. No other member of the company had a benefit at any time. Yet by a rather singular anomaly, when an old-time tragedian William Creswick, to whom Irving had no particular obligation, bade farewell at Drury Lane in 1885, the vast programme included Irving and his company in the second act of Louis XI, which must also have necessitated one of the heavy Lyceum sets being taken across the road to Drury Lane and back again.[6]

In the period of decline in the 1880's, we come upon some interesting transitional positions along the road to the purely charitable benefit. When the benefit had ceased to be a normal contractual right, it was still used as a special award for merit. We read of an actor Frank Thornton, who created a not very important part in Patience in 1881, that 'at the conclusion of that play the management tendered him the compliment of a benefit.'[7] The wheel had come full circle and Mr Thornton was singled out in 1881 just as Mrs Barry had been in 1686.

By this time the remains of the system were very much open to abuse, and when the irresponsible comedian Arthur Roberts had lost £5,000 in a disastrous managerial venture at the Royalty, he decided it was time he had a benefit, and persuaded the manage-

[5] George Raymond, op. cit., p. 394, and Oxford Companion to the Theatre, (s.v. Cooke, T.P.).

[6] Clement Scott and Cecil Howard, op. cit., II, 577 note.

[7] E. Reid and H. Compton, op. cit., p. 216.

ment of the next burlesque he played in to accord him one. This took place at the Opera Comique in the middle of 1891 'when a programme of wondrous magnitude was seen', but as the chronicler drily puts it, 'whether he was a fitting recipient for a benefit was freely discussed.'[8]

This was not the first case of a benefit deemed improper on much the same grounds. In 1847 Macready had fulminated to his diary at the news that the friends of Mr Calcraft, a former manager of the Dublin theatre, were about to get up a benefit for him.

> The propriety of this is surely questionable, when in many cases his debts were incurred with the knowledge they never could be paid, and when many, many of his indigent performers have been wanting the bread that he has taken care not to want. *This is not right.*[9]

But against Macready's censorious judgment it must be said that the Committee for this benefit of Calcraft's was headed by Lords Rathdown, Gort, Massereene, Muskerry and Talbot de Malahide, who may be presumed to know where their credit could fairly be committed.[10]

Much the same objection could have been taken thirty years later, though it does not appear to have been, in the case of F. B. Chatterton. When this weak but likeable man went bankrupt in 1879, after having managed Drury Lane for ten years, his liabilities were £36,000. 'But he had made many friends, and several benefits were arranged to aid him.'[11]

Another benefit that was questioned, not on the grounds of the unworthiness but the prosperity of the beneficiary, was that for Alfred Wigan in 1876. A theatrical writer of the time grumbles, 'Benefit to Alfred Wigan — what for? no one could tell — Alfred Wigan by his talents having retired on a handsome competency into private life.'[12]

One of the last remaining strongholds of the system was the annual provincial pantomime.* Some of these pantomimes, as is still

---

* See note on p. 25.

[8] *Ibid.*, p. 177.
[9] *Macready's Diaries*, II, 371.
[10] *History of the Theatre Royal, Dublin*, pp. 117, 118.
[11] Clement Scott and Cecil Howard, *op. cit.*, II, 586 note.
[12] Edward Stirling, *op. cit.*, I, 309.

the custom in certain parts of the North of England, ran right through till Easter, and with the continuity of performance by an unvaried company and the consequent creation and prominence of popular local favourites, more nearly reproduced the atmosphere of the old stock company days than could be the case with touring companies staying only for a week. For instance at Newcastle in 1876 in *Puss in Boots*, Emily Cross, who played Happy Harry, took her benefit on the penultimate night, a Friday, 'under the distinguished patronage of many well-known folk, headed by the Earl Percy'[13] — powerful support in Newcastle.

The potential beneficiary who came off worst during the decline was the provincial manager, whose benefit, or perhaps that of his wife, had usually been the biggest of the season. His resource seems to have been to fall back upon a benefit performance by the local amateurs as the most stable theatrical element in the uninterested cycle of weekly touring companies. There are instances of this at Dublin in 1867 and North Shields in 1884.[14]

In the 1870's another little snobbery crept in, and such benefits as still took place began to be termed 'complimentary' benefits. This affectation was greatly to the disgust of the older hands: Edward Stirling deals sarcastically with it and ends 'A benefit means a pecuniary advantage, not the courtesy of a compliment.'[15] But within a few years there seems to have been even reluctance to use the word benefit at all, and Emily Soldene at the Gaiety in 1873 primly says, 'At the end of the season Messrs Hollingshead and Morton kindly placed the theatre at my disposal for a matinée.'[16]

Miss Soldene's benefit that she did not like to call by its name also introduces the other principal change that came with the ebbing of the whole system—the morning or matinée benefit. Alfred Wigan's farewell benefit at Drury Lane in 1872, under the patronage of 'the Prince and Princess of Wales and a great number of the nobility,'[17] to which reference has already been made, was also a "morning performance". The new custom had two points to commend it. The management was relieved of the loss of a night's profit, and this

---

[13] Harold Oswald, *op. cit.*, p. 121.
[14] *History of the Theatre Royal, Dublin*, p. 171, and Robert King, *op. cit.*, pp. 113, 114.
[15] Edward Stirling, *op. cit.*, I, 308.
[16] Emily Soldene, *My Theatrical and Musical Recollections*, London, 1897, p. 137.
[17] Clement Scott and Cecil Howard, *op. cit.*, II, 414.

advantaged especially Drury Lane, under a virtual obligation to house the farewells of distinguished retiring veterans. The player, though normally an afternoon would not yield so great a receipt as an evening performance, was able, at least in London, to build up a much stronger benefit-bill, other artists, themselves playing in the evening, being available to give support at a matinée.

On the last day of the season at the Lyceum in July 1874, H. L. Bateman, Henry Irving's predecessor in the management of the theatre, went one better, and accorded himself a double benefit extending over both the matinée and evening performances on that day. The bill, as was not unusual at the time, consisted of an act from each of the notable successes of the season, Act IV of *Leah* with Miss Bateman, Act III of *The Bells*, Act IV of *Charles I*, Act II of *Philip*, all with Irving, and the farce of *Raising the Wind* with Irving as Jeremy Diddler.[18]

By 1882 so firmly was the custom established that J. H. Barnes acted Macbeth for the first time on any stage at Drury Lane for his benefit at a matinée and to a crowded house, which would have been unthinkable twenty years earlier.[19]

Miss Elizabeth Robins, a pioneer actress in Ibsen's plays, writing of 1889 when the Norwegian dramatist had just burst upon London, and when she herself was friendly with Geneviève Ward, a tragedienne very much of the old school, has an amusing story of when Mrs Beringer, desiring to arrange a benefit for her daughter Vera then playing in *Little Lord Fauntleroy,* had had the temerity to ask Miss Ward to play Mrs Alving in *Ghosts* for this benefit. After detailing Geneviève Ward's preliminary indignation, she writes:

> All the same Miss Ward was too loyally of the old school not to regard a player's Benefit as an honourable institution which called for the support of the Profession. Mr Vernon and she had recognized Mrs Beringer's business acumen in being first to take advantage of the absurd craze created by *The Doll's House* "while it lasts". There was, they admitted one play by the queer creature fit for decent people to touch—*The Pillars of Society*.[20]

And so the story continues, but it is an engaging point that not even the wicked Ibsen could stop an old-timer helping at the benefit of a friend.

[18] *Ibid.,* II, 440 and note.
[19] *Ibid.,* II, 539.
[20] Elizabeth Robins, *Both Sides of the Curtain,* London, 1940, p. 198.

PART II
THE "NIGHT"

X—PATRONAGE AND SALE OF TICKETS

THE TWO CENTURIES COVERED by the benefit system were an age in which patronage flourished in the most diverse forms. Nowhere was its intangible protection more sought after than in the theatre. On a benefit night there were anything from a couple of hundred to four thousand seats to be disposed of, usually at enhanced prices, and experience showed that nothing could dispose of them faster than the interest, awe and curiosity aroused by the intended presence of the "big wigs" in the boxes, ranging according to theatrical circumstances and degrees from Royalty to the Squire and his family.

Royalty, of course, had unchallenged supremacy, but it was on the whole rare for Royalty to attend the benefits of individual players. For some reason not discernible at this distance of time, George II attended the benefit of Madame Auretti at Drury Lane.[1] Mrs Bellamy claims that in 1751 the Prince and Princess of Wales were to have attended her benefit at Covent Garden, though prevented by the onset of the Prince's last illness.[2] Tate Wilkinson goes to the trouble of disproving her story by dates and facts, including the pertinent one that she was not playing at Covent Garden in that year,[3] but the interesting point remains from the story that, if Royalty attended a benefit, this then became a "command" and the Royal personage selected the principal play. But in such a case the destination of the receipts of the night remained in dispute; the limited evidence on so obscure and unusual a point goes to show that at least one actor came off better than one author. When the King happened to command a play on Lee Lewes's benefit night, it seems at first to have been assumed that the benefit would be postponed. But an altercation ensued when

> he remonstrated with Mr Colman, then manager, on the injustice of his night being put off on that account . . . Mr Colman, though naturally liberal, treated him on the occasion rather cavalierly, and asked him with a sneering laugh, what he would have him do? 'Should he send to the King, and desire him not

[1] Tate Wilkinson, *Memoirs of His Own Life*, III, 181.
[2] *Life of George Anne Bellamy*, II, 623.
[3] Tate Wilkinson, *Memoirs of His Own Life*, III, 204.

to come, because it was Lee Lewes's night?' 'No, Sir?' said Lewes very spiritedly, 'but I shall expect the receipt of the house on that night.'[4]

Charles Dibdin was less fortunate, for by 1780 when his equivalent case arose, he had made too much of a habit of speaking 'very spiritedly' to his managers, so he received no satisfaction, and had to write in his autobiography

> by theatrical prescription, an author cannot have a concern in any night when the King commands; and the King having commanded the *Islanders* on the sixth night, I was compelled to take my proportion of the tenth, by which exaction I lost above fifty pounds.[5]

The most notable example of Royalty honouring a player fell to the lot of that pillar of Victorian propriety and despiser of the profession he led, William Charles Macready. On the occasion of his impending departure for America in 1848, a special performance was given at Drury Lane; this was not only "by special command" of Queen Victoria, but it was also by her command that the performance was for Macready's own benefit. The Queen and the Prince Consort attended in State with other members of the Royal Family, and the performance cleared about £1,200.[6] An interesting aspect of the etiquette of Royal theatregoing emerged. The pit and galleries being overcrowded, there was some disturbance at first; Macready, desiring to offer their money back to those who wished to go, 'sent to ask leave to address the audience', and when the Queen had granted this, he soon put the matter right.

John O'Keeffe the dramatist, when old, blind, ill and poor, was given a benefit at Covent Garden in 1800. This was under the patronage of the Prince of Wales, the Duke and Duchess of York, the Duke of Clarence and the Duke of Cumberland—a galaxy of Royal patrons. The beneficiary objected to being described in the bill as 'The Unfortunate Author', but was pacified by assurances that this referred only to his blindness.[7]

The nature of the general rule against Royalty attending individual benefits is shown in the letter Charles Young received before

---

[4] John Williams ("Anthony Pasquin"), *op. cit.*, II, 147.
[5] *The Professional Life of Mr Dibdin*, II, 68.
[6] *Macready's Diaries*, II, 399-401.
[7] *Recollections of the Life of John O'Keeffe*, II, 384, and Garrick Club Playbill Collection.

his farewell benefit in 1832 from the Comptroller to the Duchess of
Kent, Queen Victoria's mother.

. . . although her Royal Highness does not, from motives which
he can easily understand, go to benefits, that she may avoid
showing preferences, yet, *on this occasion,* where it is a farewell
one, her Royal Highness is anxious to show the interest she
takes in the drama of this country, as also, *especially,* to evince
the same feeling towards Mr Young, in recollection of the many
occasions on which she has been gratified by his admirable
representations.[8]

But any connection with the Court would relax this rule and when
George Bartley's farewell benefit in 1852 was 'under the immediate
patronage of her Majesty and his Royal Highness Prince Albert,'
this seems to have been because Bartley had at one time been
selected to give lessons in elocution to the Prince of Wales.[9]

Other exceptions to the rule that Royalty rarely patronized
individual benefits are provided by the theatres in those towns where
Royalty unbent in the enjoyment of family life and holiday mood.
Such places were primarily Windsor, Weymouth, Brighton and
Richmond, occasionally Plymouth and Portsmouth, as ports of call
on George III's yachting cruises.

At Windsor, where the present Royal Family is very well
acquainted with the Theatre Royal, George III went constantly to
the theatre. In 1800 he commanded Bannister's benefit there,
naming the plays he wanted to see,[10] and the year before he had
commanded five out of six of Elliston's Windsor performances, and
being unable to attend the benefit, sent 25 guineas as a contribution.[11] At Weymouth, during his annual summer visit, the King
seems to have attended the benefits as a matter of course, and once,
when due to return to London to open Parliament, he actually
agreed to drive all through the night, in order to be able before his
departure to attend the benefit of an actor named Goddard.[12]

Brighton gained similar favoured treatment from the time that
George IV, when Prince of Wales, established a residence there. In
1786 the Prince bespoke the benefit play of the manager John

8 Julian Young, *op. cit.,* I, 115.
9 John Cole, *op. cit.,* II, 44-46.
10 John Adolphus, *op. cit.,* II, 59.
11 George Raymond, *op. cit.,* p. 52.
12 Walter Donaldson, *op. cit.,* pp. 116, 117.

Bernard, and a courtier 'came to take all the boxes, which occasioned the elevation of the pit to the box prices.'[13] A later manager,
Brunton, had a daughter Louise (afterwards Countess of Craven),
who was his leading lady, and her benefit was honoured in the
successive years of 1805 and 1806 by the presence of the Prince, who
in the former year brought the Duke of Orleans with him.[14] At a
later date Royal Princesses also extended benefit patronage, and in
1834 Princess Augusta patronized the benefit of the Brighton box
office keeper, which, no doubt, accounted for his bill including the
band of the 1st Dragoons.[15]

Richmond gained from the proximity of the Duke of Clarence
and Mrs Jordan at Bushey Park and the Duke and Duchess of
Cumberland at Kew, all being frequent visitors, while Mrs Jordan
played there from time to time.[16]

But though Royal patronage was the apogee of benefit hopes, the
exercise of care, tact and straightforward dealings were called for,
as Royal frowns could be disastrous. Writing of that persistent
theatregoer George III at Windsor, a member of the company
reported

> I learnt, that the year before his Majesty had condescended to
> command a play for the benefit of the whole company; but it
> coming to his knowledge that they were not satisfied with the
> division of the house—the manager having thought proper to
> include some performers in it as sharers, who had, but did not
> at that time belong to the theatre—there was little hope of that
> honour ever being granted again.[17]

After Royalty, Dukes, Duchesses and the rest of the then very
limited nobility—the number of peers did not exceed 200 until about
1820—came next in the heirarchy of desired benefit patrons. At her
first benefit about 1744, George Anne Bellamy was fortunate enough
to attract the attention of the formidable and powerful Duchess of
Queensberry, so the occupants of her boxes also included the
Duchess Dowager of Leeds, and the Countesses of Cardigan and
Shaftesbury.[18]

13 John Bernard, *op. cit.*, II, 71.
14 H. C. Porter, *op. cit.*, p. 23.
15 *Ibid.*, p. 63.
16 Edward Stirling, *op. cit.*, I, 200.
17 E. C. Everard, *op. cit.*, p. 152.
18 *Life of George Anne Bellamy*, I, 63, 64.

The record as a patroness of the actress Harriot Mellon, successively wife of the banker Thomas Coutts and of the Duke of St Albans (respectively a great deal older and a great deal younger than herself), is inconsistent. In 1821 at Brighton a Mrs Gibbs, described as 'a favourite Surrey actress', took her benefit, and it is related that 'Although Mr and Mrs Thomas Coutts declined to patronise Mrs Gibbs's benefit, they bought £85 worth of tickets.'[19] As £90 to £100 was a good benefit house at Brighton at this period, no doubt Mrs Gibbs would have forgiven this curious little piece of snobbery. Yet seven years later we find the starchy Duchess of St Albans extending her patronage to the benefit of Mrs Waylett, whose reputation was unmistakably bad.[20]

Palpably an intending bénéficiaire could have no more powerful noble support than that of the Lord Chamberlain himself, more particularly in the years prior to 1843 when the "minor" theatres, those other than Drury Lane and Covent Garden, operated, if licensed at all, upon a licence that restricted the months of their performance as well as confining them to "burlettas". As a rule no benefits were taken at the Olympic under Madame Vestris's management, but in 1830, however,

> Mrs Glover applied to the Lord Chamberlain, the Duke of Devonshire, for an extra night beyond that for which the theatre was licensed, and through her influence in that quarter, obtained it, and took a benefit on the ensuing Easter Monday . . . on this occasion the company without exception gave their services gratuitously, out of respect to the kind-hearted lady and "mother of the theatre" as she was familiarly called.[21]

It was perhaps something of a declension from the higher nobility to such as Lord Mayors, but these had their value when they behaved as expansively as did Sir Watkin Lewis, Lord Mayor of London in 1781. Miss Phillips (afterwards Mrs Crouch) was a Welsh girl, and had used this link to lure her compatriot from the Mansion House to her benefit at Drury Lane.

> In the stage-box, left of the pit sat Sir Watkin Lewis, with his gold chain as Lord Mayor, the Lady Mayoress, and a large party. Many of the other boxes were nobly, and all were

19 H. C. Porter, *op. cit.*, p. 49.
20 *Ibid.*, p. 58.
21 Malcolm Mackintosh (The Old Stager), *op. cit.*, p. 74.

elegantly filled . . . The Lord Mayor, when the opera was ended, sent for Mr Phillips into his box, and both his lordship and the Lady Mayoress kindly congratulated him on the merit and success of his daughter.[22]

There is one curious case of what might be termed negative patronage. Ned Shuter, the comedian, was of an intensely religious turn of mind, and normally attended Chapel four times on Sunday. In consequence, Whitfield, though an inveterate opponent of the Theatre, granted his Nonconformist flock a dispensation to attend Shuter's benefit.[23]

In the provinces patronage made itself felt at the box-office in an even more pronounced way.

When only sixteen in 1777, Mrs Jordan's benefit at Cork proved a complete failure from want of patronage; but the young bucks were on her side: by riotous conduct they procured her another benefit, and this brought in a welcome £40.[24] Twenty-five years later, she played on her autumn tour at Margate, where the Duchess of Devonshire was staying. She wrote back to the Duke of Clarence,

I thought proper (as the Duchess of Devonshire sent to know how long I stayd) to let her know that my night was fixed for Friday, on which she sent me the most civil letter, highly pleased with the attention, desiring me to keep both stage boxes & if her name would be any use, to *say by her* DESIRE.[25]

At Brighton noble patrons were as thick as blackberries, and in the single year of 1806 individual benefits there were patronized by the Prince of Wales, the Duke of Marlborough, the Marchioness of Downshire, the Earl of Craven and Lady Anna Wyndham.[26]

But the greatly desired patronage of the nobility might have its less agreeable side. Henry Lee, a West Country manager, playing in Wales in 1797, obtained the patronage of the Marquis of Lansdowne, but the patron said that 'on account of his age and infirmities' he should have to leave before the end of the entertainments. The courteous old peer added 'You will, I hope apologize for me to your performers', but there was the risk that the audience might interpret as displeasure the early departure of the magnate.[27]

[22] M. J. Young, *op. cit.*, I, 101, 104.
[23] G. T. Watts, *Theatrical Bristol*, Bristol, 1915, p. 93.
[24] John Fyvie, *op. cit.*, pp. 358, 359.
[25] A. Aspinall, *op. cit.*, pp. 50, 51.
[26] H. C. Porter, *op. cit.*, pp. 23-25.
[27] Henry Lee, *Memoirs of A Manager*, Taunton, 1830, I, 178, 179.

Some ten years later at Banff, the Earl of Fife was very frank indeed to Everard, when the latter called 'to solicit the honour of his name and patronage for my benefit.'

> He condescended to tell me that I might have it, but added, that he thought I should do better without it; 'For' said his lordship to me, 'I am sorry to say, that small as our town is, we are somewhat divided; — if you are patronized by one party, the other won't come; — let it alone, and you'll have us all.'[28]

At Swansea in 1786 'our theatre was crowded for the benefit of Mr Calvert, the proprietor, with as brilliant an audience as was even seen in so small a circle. There were no less than twelve titles present, besides many families of the first distinction.'[29]

The memoirs of the smaller provincial players contain numerous proud and pathetic gloatings over patronage obtained and its results. Mrs Holbrook and her husband at Cheltenham in 1807 'had the good fortune to be noticed by the Right Honourable Countess Kenmare, who patronised our benefit, and fixed on *John Bull.*'[30] Robert Dyer had been in low water at Plymouth in 1828, but 'under the patronage of Lord Boringdon my benefit reached nearly £120.'[31] At York in 1764 Tate Wilkinson was pleased enough that his benefit was 'by desire of Col. Thornton,'[32] but next year at Doncaster he stepped up on this, for his benefit 'was particularly honoured, with not only being very full, but all the genteel families came on that occasion to our little theatre; and no wonder, for besides the compliment paid me, Sir George Coke's mother . . . did me the honour unasked to patronize my play.'[33]

The naval or military hero of the hour was a wonderful benefit card during the Napoleonic Wars if he would make what is now called a "personal appearance". Sir Sydney Smith 'after his long durance and miraculous escape' (presumably, therefore, in 1798) did this at Bath.

> An old actor with a large family having a benefit, he gave his permission to announce that he would attend the theatre. His

[28] E. C. Everard, *op. cit.*, p. 133.
[29] Cecil Price, *op. cit.*, p. 82.
[30] Mrs Holbrook, *Memoirs of an Actress*, Manchester, 1807, p. 25.
[31] Robert Dyer, *Nine Years of an Actor's Life,* London and Plymouth, 1833, p. 58.
[32] Tate Wilkinson, *Memoirs of His Own Life,* III, 37.
[33] *Ibid.,* III, 108.

condescension put a clear hundred pounds in the pocket of a worthy man, who else, as usual, might not have gained five pounds.[34]

The teller of this story was nearer the mark than he may have known in suggesting that Sir Sydney's motive was 'to gratify the longing people with a sight of him,' this officer having a publicity sense greatly in advance of his day.

The hero of the hour in a more limited sphere could also be a politician, and at Warwick in the early 19th century the same provincial player wrote 'luckily for me, my benefit falling on the day after Sir George Shuckburgh was elected, I obtained the honour of his name and patronage.'[35]

It is altogether typical of Edmund Kean that when he had obtained the necessary patronage for his benefit at Exeter in 1813, he should at once resent it. His patroness was Mrs Buller of Downes, and unfortunately Kean met the lady's butler, who remarked 'You will be sure to have a good house, as my mistress patronizes the play.' Kean at once vowed that he would not trouble to sell a single ticket, saying 'If the people would not come to see my acting, it shan't be said they came by Mrs Buller's desire.'[36]

The crying need for social patronage inevitably brought some trickery with it. An actor named Lamash—he was the original Trip in *The School for Scandal*—playing in Edinburgh in the early years of the 19th century, hit upon the simple device of instructing his wife to spread the story that she was the daughter of an Irish peer. 'Lamash and his wife were in consequence highly patronized and their benefit was abundantly productive.'[37]

If all patronage failed, the classic phrase placed at the head of the bill in a pathetic attempt to conceal the social nakedness of the land, was "By particular Desire of Several Persons of Distinction." Within the profession this soon became a mocking catchword.[38]

When local magnates were not available the Services could be relied upon to patronize benefits in addition to the bespeaks that were regularly desired by the officers of regiments in garrison towns,

[34] E. C. Everard, *op. cit.*, pp. 169, 170.

[35] *Ibid.*, p. 101.

[36] William Cotton, *op. cit.*, p. 31.

[37] George Raymond, *op. cit.*, p. 407.

[38] John Adolphus, *op. cit.*, I, 384. For this point see also the famous farce about strollers, *Sylvester Daggerwood*, by George Colman, Jr, 1795.

and, less frequently, by the officers of warships in seaports. At Brighton, for instance, the 55th Regiment patronized Mrs Glover in 1800, and the 6th Iniskillen Dragoons did the same to Munyard in 1844.[39] In such cases the Band of the Regiment would generally take part. The support was all the heartier if an old comrade were in any way concerned. Joe Cowell, the comedian, had been a Midshipman in the Royal Navy for three years, and when in 1812 at the end of his first season on the stage, at the Dock Theatre, Plymouth, he took his benefit, though he was naturally quite a junior member of the company, it was 'By desire of the officers of his majesty's ship *York* . . . nearly the whole of the crew, the band at their head and the marines bringing up the rear, marched to the theatre.'[40]

The presence of sailors was in itself an additional attraction, as Mrs Holbrook found at Gosport in 1807 when her benefit was 'patronized by several officers of his Majesty's ships that fought in the glorious action off Trafalgar; and as the bespeak of the gallant tars was to the ladies irresistable, it turned out very lucrative.'[41]

Military patronage was steadier than naval, if perhaps less heartily enthusiastic through all parts of the house, though some curious but effective inducements to benefit patronage by the other ranks were offered. Mrs Waylett was a lady of definitely amorous propensities, and was described as 'a great favourite with the officers of the regiment then stationed in Belfast' when she was in that city about 1826 or 1827. So these gentlemen

> resolved to support her benefit to the extent of their power, and a bumper house they made of it for her. All of their men who bought tickets were allowed leave of absence from barracks until midnight, and in consequence the audience was mainly a military one.[42]

But even in military patronage there were risks to be run. In November 1840 a benefit performance at the Theatre Royal, Brighton, was announced as being 'under the patronage of the Right Honourable the Lieutenant-Colonel the Earl of Cardigan and the officers of the 11th Hussars', but as Lord Cardigan was at that time an object of public execration about a court-martial in his

[39] H. C. Porter, *op. cit.*, pp. 21, 81.
[40] Joe Cowell, *op. cit.*, p. 21.
[41] Mrs Holbrook, *op. cit.*, p. 30.
[42] Malcolm Mackintosh (The Old Stager), *op. cit.*, p. 44.

Regiment, his appearance in the theatre was greeted by the audience with hisses, yells and groans.

This collective military patronage can seldom have extended to the totally different conditions prevailing in the metropolis, but about 1843 for his benefit at the Princess's Theatre, the comedian Paul Bedford 'obtained the patronage of my Lord Combermere and officers of the First Life Guards', which was distinctly a feat.[43]

The latest date that has been noted for collective military patronage is 1882, a date that is very late indeed, the whole benefit system being on its last legs by then. Yet at North Shields in that year, the benefit of Miss Adeline Stanhope in *The Beautiful Russian* was under the patronage of Captain Rowlandson and the Officers of the King's Own (Royal Lancaster) Regiment. One imagines a bored detachment in command of a Captain, pleased enough to revive one of the customs of an earlier day.[44]

In Dublin, always a law to itself in theatrical matters, the custom of the social patronage of benefit nights was carried to curious lengths in the 18th century.

> Leading actors attached themselves to some lady of quality, who took on herself the management of his 'night', canvassed her acquaintances, disposed of tickets, and received the fashionable part of the audience in the box-room, as though she were the hostess. The night was called, not the actor's but 'Lady . . . 's night', and there was a sort of emulation among them, to have their particular 'night' successful.[45]

But there is a cautionary tale in this connection. In 1758 a certain *parvenue*, being ambitious of trying her strength against the higher grades, was rash enough to take a patronizing lead for the benefit of some actor. The fashionables decided to snub her and did not turn up, leaving her boxes empty; her chagrin was doubled by the box-keeper, who kept coming to her to say 'Your ladyship's gallery is excellent . . . your ladyship's pit improves' and similar galling words of intended encouragement.[46] The Viceroy adopted the Royal attitude of not patronizing individual benefits as a rule, but his rare patronage was given in 1753 when, after the theatre in Dublin had been virtually destroyed in a series of riots, it was reopened with

---

[43] *Recollections of Paul Bedford*, London, 1867, p. 79.
[44] Robert King, *op. cit.*, p. 110.
[45] Percy Fitzgerald, *Life of David Garrick*, I, 176.
[46] George Raymond, *op. cit.*, pp. 166, 167.

Peg Woffington's benefit night,[47] and in 1818 the generally popular Fanny Kelly managed to secure the tribute of a Viceregal command upon her night.[48]

Something not very far removed from the Dublin custom prevailed for a period in London also. After the Duchess of Queensberry had given her patronage to George Anne Bellamy's benefit about 1744, the actress in the green room

> was accosted by Prince Lobkowitz, who was here in a public character, requesting a box at my benefit for the *corps diplomatique*. After thanking his Highness for the honour intended me, I informed him that they might be accommodated with a stage box; and sending for the house-keeper, desired he would make an entry in his book to this purpose. But how great was my surprise when he acquainted me I had not a box to dispose of; every one . . . (except three in other hands) . . . being retained for Her Grace the Duchess of Queensberry . . . and further added that the Duchess had likewise sent for two hundred and fifty tickets.[49]

Apart from bespeaks, which are dealt with in Chapter III, there are some instances of collective civilian patronage of an individual benefit. During the Regency period a beneficiary at Exeter obtained unsolicited the

> patronage of the ladies and gentlemen of the Crescent, consisting then, I think of about fifteen of some of the first houses in Exeter; they were, of course, connected and acquainted with the first families in the city, and without doubt intended on this occasion to use their interest.[50]

Another case of collective patronage of a benefit, and one with a charmingly human touch, is provided by a happening at Norwich in 1852. A popular actor named Phillips had an accident in *Rob Roy* owing to the collapse of a bridge, and fractured a leg in April 1851. Next year, when his benefit came round this was 'under the immediate patronage of the medical staff of the Norfolk and Norwich Hospital'.[51]

[47] Janet Camden Lucey, *op. cit.*, p. 181.
[48] Basil Francis, *op. cit.*, p. 79.
[49] *Life of George Anne Bellamy*, I, pp. 63, 64.
[50] E. C. Everard, *op. cit.*, p. 163.
[51] Bosworth Harcourt, *op. cit.*, p. 63.

Freemasons, in addition to theatrical patronage by the bespeaking of nights, often gave collective patronage to a beneficiary who was a brother of their Craft; the benefit of Davis, the Newcastle manager in 1849, was under the patronage of six separate Masonic Lodges.[52]

Vying in importance with the actual sale of boxes and seats were the personal presents of money made to artists at their benefits by patrons and admirers. These were known in the earlier 18th century as "guineas" or "guinea tickets" and in the later 18th century as "gold tickets". The late Mr W. J. Lawrence thought that this custom traced its origin to fashionable people always making all payments in gold[53]—the modern equivalent might quite well be the signing of the bill in a smart restaurant—and this idea of payments in gold is born out by the account of Mrs Bellamy's benefit already mentioned, when the Duchess of Queensberry also gave the young actress a hundred and fifty guineas with the proud words 'Queensberry can give no person less than gold.'[54] While "guineas" could be of any amount, "gold tickets" are mostly spoken of as if they were in multiples of £50. Mrs Bellamy mentions them in connection with two of her subsequent benefits, at one of which 'Lord Kildare, Lord Granby, Mr Fox and Mr Digby . . . took four tickets at one hundred pounds each.'[55] At the other 'my great gold tickets, however, failed. For I received but one hundred from Lord Holderness; fifty a piece from General Monkton, Lord Granby and Lord Pigot; and one fifty in a blank cover, which I have often suspected came from Mr Woodward.'[56]

Tate Wilkinson in 1758 at Dublin[57] had 'gold tickets to a considerable amount, not only from my friends and some persons of distinction, but particularly from the gentlemen of the army.'*

* 'As the word ticket, in this connection, seems to imply a right of admission as well as a donation, it is rather more than possible that a gold admission token was issued to contributors of gold tickets.' So Troubridge: but compare, for instance, Tate Wilkinson, The Wandering Patentee, III, 244: 'Mrs Jordan was also disappointed, I believe, as to gold tickets, for except one lady five guineas, I do not believe she had any presents'—which equally seems to suggest that a gold ticket was only a slang theatre phrase, and not more visible than a golden opinion. Certainly no such tokens have ever been found. V.C.C-B.

[52] Harold Oswald, op. cit., p. 51.
[53] W. J. Lawrence, Old Theatre Days and Ways, London, 1935, p. 189.
[54] Life of George Anne Bellamy, I, 63, 64.
[55] Ibid., II, 199, 200.
[56] Ibid., IV, 58, 59.
[57] Tate Wilkinson, Memoirs of His Own Life, I, 172, 173.

At her second benefit at Drury Lane in 1783 Mrs Siddons received 90 guineas from Lady Spencer for her side box, and from Lady Aylesbury a bank note of £50 for an upper box.[58] Harriot Mellon, an actress who became, by her first marriage to Mr Coutts the banker, one of the richest women of her time, met her first husband when he sent her five freshly minted guineas for a box at her benefit at Cheltenham in 1805, with the hope that his 'trifling present' would become 'luck money', which it did indeed to the lady.[59] The purchase of a single box could have a less innocent significance. In 1821 Fanny Kelly considered, probably with every justice, that Lord Yarmouth had designs upon her virtue, so when he sent her £200 for a box at her benefit, she returned the draft.[60]

One reference to a benefit of Mrs Siddons at Edinburgh in 1785 adds the words 'Presents by plate and gold tickets could not amount to less than 120 l.'[61] This is the only reference the writer knows of to presents of plate at a normal benefit, though such a presentation might be made to a retiring manager.

The custom of giving presents, "guineas" or "gold tickets" at benefits began to die away after 1820, in which year the austere Macready, destined to be the leader of the profession in another fifteen years, set his face against it. The year before at Edinburgh, on being sent a guinea for a box-ticket of his benefit night, he had returned it, saying 'it was not my practice to receive presents on my benefit night.' [62] In 1820 he made a public stand, considering the question to be involved with that raising of the status of the former rogues and vagabonds that culminated in Irving's knighthood in 1895. He wrote in his reminiscences

> This custom seems to me to compromise the actor's independence, and in that belief I had laid it down as a rule not to accept more than the value of the ticket required ... I could not consider myself sitting down to table on terms of social equality with a man to whom I had been obliged for the gift of five, ten or twenty pounds.[63]

At the farewell benefit at the Queens in 1868 of Paul Bedford, the low comedian, E. L. Blanchard, theatrical critic and gossip writer,

[58] James Boaden, *Life of Mrs Siddons*, II, 2.
[59] John Fyvie, *op. cit.*, pp. 412, 413.
[60] Basil Francis, *op. cit.*, pp. 103, 104.
[61] John Jackson, *op. cit.*, p. 129.
[62] W. C. Macready, *Reminiscences*, I, 181.
[63] *Ibid.*, I, 215.

reports 'a great house, as I hear about £700, including presents of money.'[64] This is a rather late date for "presents of money", and shows the persistence of the old "gold ticket" system, forty-seven years after Macready, as head of the profession, had rejected it. It might perhaps also be argued that the comedians, less encumbered by attitudes and principles, tended to preserve custom longer than their tragic brethren.

A benefit was also a proper occasion upon which reparation could be made for a wrong or injustice. When in 1775 those charged with riot and conspiracy on the occasion of the riot against Macklin two years earlier, were placed on trial, the actor did not wish to press the charges. The Judge approved the terms of compensation suggested by Macklin, which were that the defendants should take £100 worth of tickets for his benefit, £100 worth for his daughter's benefit and £100 worth for one of the manager's nights on which he played.[65] Similarly, when about 1830 an actress called Mrs Waylett suffered under a libel that her mode of life rendered tempting, in addition to a written apology, 'the parties implicated sent Mrs Waylett £50 for a ticket, in case her benefit might suffer by the scurrility.'[66]

It was in something of the same spirit that when the then manager of the Surrey Theatre in 1881 had been threatened with a pistol by a drunken and aggrieved dramatist, George Conquest remarked 'It's a great pity he didn't wound you, Bill. What a splendid benefit you could have got out of it.'[67]

With the box-office as a permanent intermediary, so to speak, the balance of demand for benefit tickets caused a position in which a star would receive applications for tickets either from the intending purchaser in person or through a servant, at his own house, while "small people" had to sally out into the city and sell their tickets as best they could. The position varied with the period and the social standing of the purchaser. George Anne Bellamy, of course, waited on the Duchess of Queensberry at her house. Mrs Wells went to Elliston's house to buy a ticket for his benefit—'I waited on him for a ticket, for which he received the money',[68] and she was mightily aggrieved that a fellow artist should have to do such a thing.

The opposite rule of the actor calling on his patrons was not

[64] Clement Scott and Cecil Howard, op. cit., II, 360 and note.
[65] R. B. Peake, op. cit., I, 341, 342.
[66] Amatory Biograph of Mrs Waylett, London, n.d., [c. 1831] p. 11.
[67] Frances Fleetwood, op. cit., p. 144.
[68] Life of Mrs Sumbel, late Wells, written by Herself, II, 215.

altogether inviolable. When Yates took his benefit at Goodman's Fields Theatre to the East of the City, he somewhat impertinently advertised the impossibility of his calling personally on theatrical patrons in the neighbourhood, on the ground that he had got into such a strange part of the town, he could not find his way about the streets.[69] At Cardiff about 1822 one of the actors advertised before a benefit night that he had hurt his foot and was unable to pay his respects to the gentry in person, an indication that the old custom of soliciting the purchase of benefit tickets cap in hand still persisted then.[70]

"Gentleman" Lewis, who was stage-manager of Covent Garden for twenty years prior to 1809, never had tickets at his benefit. He was enabled to dispense with the anxiety and organization involved, as, by stipulation his post carried with it the right to a benefit on the last night before Passion-week, the best night in the season.[71]

The biography of the tragedian Charles Mayne Young reproduces the detailed box-office return of his farewell benefit at Covent Garden in 1832, and this presents some points of interest. There were 2,975 persons in a house of £643-7-6. Of these, 592 came in on tickets issued and sold by Young, paying £207-4-0, while 2,383 paid £436-3-6 at the doors. Young's tickets included 580 of the 1,007 seats in the boxes. The principle disclosed, perhaps more pronounced than usual at a farewell, is that if the beneficiary could take care of half the boxes, representing about a third of the house in money, the rest of the house would take care of itself on a big benefit occasion.[72]

When artists had a benefit to make, they would, especially if they were singers, frequent the meetings of Philanthropic Societies, described as 'a kind of offset from the Masons.' They would have their benefit tickets in their pockets, and the calling upon one of them for a song in the course of the "harmony of the evening" would probably result in a sale taking place. Charles Dibdin the elder describes the scene. 'The song over. "Mr Beard" said a gentleman, "please to set me down for a box that will hold nine. There are two guineas and a half and half a crown".'[73] The procedure was just the same in the provinces; this is an old account from the Worcester circuit about 1780:

[69] J. Doran, *op. cit.*, pp. 397, 398.
[70] Cecil Price, *op. cit.*, p. 121.
[71] *Recollections of the Life of John O'Keeffe*, II, 296.
[72] Julian Young, *op. cit.*, I, 116.
[73] *The Professional Life of Mr. Dibdin*, I, 42, 43.

No performer during the time made a benefit fit to be so called, except our first singer; . . . Being invited to clubs and suppers, he gave them song after song, and in the moment of conviviality, got them to put down their names for a certain number of tickets, and by these means ensured a good benefit long before his time.[74]

The benefit tickets with which leading players stuffed their pockets at these times were quite elaborate affairs, and often beautifully engraved. The ticket for Munden's farewell benefit 'representd a Muse, resting upon a lyre, and displaying an open book, with the inscription "All's Well that Ends Well."'[75] Almost a century earlier the ticket for Spiller's benefit was designed by Hogarth, and is familiar from frequent reproduction.

Usually at benefits "the free list was entirely suspended" as the phrase went, but this does not seem to have been always the case during the earlier period, for in 1703, Mary Baldwin complained that at her benefit at Drury Lane 'so many free persons were admitted that she had no profit.'[76]

Our modern theatre-ticket agencies, succeeding to this part of the business that the libraries carried out in the first half of the 19th century—they are still referred to as "libraries" inside the Theatre—also had their still earlier predecessors in the coffee-houses. The announcement of Garrick's first benefit in London at Goodman's Fields in December 1742, adds 'Tickets are to be had at the Bedford Coffee-house, Tom's in Cornhill, Cary's in the Minories, at the Fleece, and at Mr Garrick's lodgings in Mansfield-street, Goodman's Fields.'[77] The fact that at benefits more than one ticket-selling agency was at work resulted inevitably from time to time in what is generally regarded as a modern theatre nuisance, the "double", when the same seats have been sold separately to two different persons. Tate Wilkinson reports that at a benefit at Hull in 1776 'a disturbance had arose' from just this very cause.[78]

The system of patronage in vogue in the provinces is clearly set out by Mrs Calvert, who is writing of the 1840's.

The custom was that the bénéficiaire should endeavour to get a

[74] E. C. Everard, *op. cit.*, p. 49.
[75] *Memoirs of J. S. Munden*, p. 290.
[76] Allardyce Nicoll, *XVIIIth Century Drama 1700-1750*, pp. 291-293.
[77] Percy Fitzgerald, *Life of David Garrick*, I, 97.
[78] Tate Wilkinson, *The Wandering Patentee*, I, 232.

patron for the occasion, whose name figured at the top of the
bill; then he issued tickets signed with his own name for pit,
gallery and dress-circle . . . These tickets were distributed in
dozens to one's friends, and to tradespeople and others, who did
their utmost to dispose of them, and felt a sort of pride in the
numbers they sold.[79]

Just like the Dublin ladies!

There were certain towns, of which Bath was one, where the
efforts of the poor players to dispose of their benefit tickets were
impeded by managerial scruples of refinement that prohibited performers from visiting or writing to solicit patronage. It was Mrs
Siddons's eye on the main chance that provided the counter to this
move, for during her seasons at Bath 1780-1782 she instituted the
placing of a book in the box-office 'for those ladies and gentlemen
to subscribe, who should wish to pay a compliment to the merits of
any of the performers, and might be absent from Bath at the time
of their benefits.'[80] This book idea she carried with her the following
year to Drury Lane, where at her first benefit 'her *book,* as it lay
open in the lobby, was literally the Court Guide.'[81]

On the still lower theatrical level of the strollers, we have an
account of what happened at the end of the 18th century. 'As soon
as the benefit was announced, Mrs Long wash'd her eight children
and dress'd them in their scarlet spencers . . . At the head of this
little tribe, she paraded the streets . . . with a large bundle of playbills, and solicited custom at every respectable dwelling.'[82]

We also learn that Mrs Siddons, in her early strolling days in her
father Roger Kemble's company, did not disdain to go round in a
red woollen cloak, knocking at each door to deliver the playbill of
her benefit.[83] The saddest story of provincial benefit-making comes
from Birmingham about 1835, when an actor at a small theatre in
the Bull-ring considered it necessary to parade the streets in
Shylock's gabardine with his dog, and a label tied round its neck
'Come and see to-night! Bow, wow! Only sixpence!'[84]

[79] Mrs Charles Calvert, *Sixty-Eight Years on the Stage,* London, 1911, p. 6.
[80] S. Penley, *op. cit.,* p. 61.
[81] James Boaden, *Life of Mrs Siddons,* II, 2.
[82] S. W. Ryley, *op. cit.,* I, 255.
[83] *Memoirs of J. S. Munden,* p. 13.
[84] Edward Stirling, *op cit.,* I, 85.

XI—MAKING UP THE BILL

THE COMPOSITION OF THE LENGTHY BENEFIT bill was of paramount importance, entailing months of consideration, cajolery and mutual deals with friendly fellow players whose support would be reflected at the box-office, and in general the advice of 'whom your wisest friends you will'.

Elaborate compliments were sometimes planned, but at least one proved double-edged. Mrs Siddons's benefit at Drury Lane in 1797 fell upon the day upon which Miss Elizabeth Farren intended to leave the stage to marry the Earl of Derby, and 'the entertainments of the bill were selected with reference to that event,' Mrs Inchbald's *The Wedding Day* being the *pièce de résistance*. But the intended kindness of Mrs Siddons and the rest of the company rather misfired; it had not been noticed until too late that the plot of Mrs Inchbald's play concerned 'an old man of rank marrying a young woman, and the return of his first wife, the day was over,' so the audience was inclined to snicker.[1]

Personal friends and good-hearted members of the company could be relied upon for additional songs and dances between the pieces, and even between the acts, with quiet arrangements and log-rollings. In 1800 Tom Dibdin provided Bannister with a new sketch for his benefit at Covent Garden, and in return Bannister played at Mrs Dibdin's night at Richmond.[2] At popular Fanny Kelly's benefit at Drury Lane in 1827, six artists 'introduced in the course of the Evening' sang twelve songs between them.[3] New songs were an attraction, but as the licenser demanded his guinea for these, their number had to be restricted. But there was no limit to the poetic afflatus of friends with literary ambitions, also well to the fore at benefits. When Miss Goward (afterwards Mrs Keeley), took her first benefit at Ipswich in 1824 at the age of 17, she recited an address, composed for her by a woman friend, beginning

[1] James Boaden, *The Life of Mrs Jordan*, I, 328.
[2] Thomas Dibdin, *op. cit.*, I, 267, 268.
[3] Basil Francis, *op. cit.*, Playbill as endpaper.

> Should I attempt in language to reveal
> The force, the tenderness of all I feel

and going on to do so for thirty-two lines.[4]

But the attractions to make up the main bill left a considerable range of choice, according to the circumstances of the artist and the theatre. The manager, both directly through the rules of the theatre and also indirectly, had a decisive say in the matter, and if he exercised his power of veto, it would probably be because of complaints (and especially from about 1825) of cramming too much into a benefit bill, for he knew that after eleven the actors were tired, and the audience became restive.[5] In the early 19th century in the provinces, this managerial power of veto on the composition of a benefit bill seems to have rested also upon another very reasonable proviso regarding the choice of pieces, expressed as 'the power of the company to enact them.' The Drury Lane artists' contract of 1826 laid down what was permissible as 'one such play or opera, and one burletta or ballet, or farce, or musical afterpiece, to be chosen out of the common stock list of acting plays.'[6] But this was a minimum, and a play, interlude and farce were generally allowed.

It must, however, be understood that the word interlude is susceptible of more than one theatrical meaning, and where, as in Wales and on the Welsh border, an interlude was a rough piece of combined miming and horseplay, more or less directly descended from mediaeval entertainment, it was regarded with aversion and contempt by managements and players alike. In the Rules of Austin and Whitlock's provincial company in the late 18th century it was laid down 'that no person whatever shall be permitted to put in the Bills of their Benefit any Interlude either Speaking or Pantomimical, as they only tend to disgrace the business in general.'[7] This was another sort of overriding rule to the manager's general right of veto over the benefit bill.

But when the manager's own benefit came round, he was inclined to forget these injunctions regarding length. At Exeter in 1788 Stephen Kemble's benefit consisted of a Prologue, a Recital, a two-act Comedy, a Recitation, an Interlude, a Farce and another

[4] Walter Goodman, *op. cit.*, pp. 91-93.
[5] J. E. Cunningham, *op. cit.*, p. 46.
[6] Thomas Leman Rede, *op. cit.*, p. 70.
[7] Cecil Price, *op. cit.*, p. 52, quoting British Museum Ms 2539 1 f 98 Burney Collection.

Comedy.[8] Managerial permission was required for a new play, and seldom withheld, even if the play were one that had already been refused by the theatre for normal production.

Broadly speaking, there were five main possibilities of a satisfactory centrepiece to the bill, which will be examined in turn. The beneficiary could put himself forward either in his popular role or in a new character different to or more important than those he normally sustained; he could obtain the services, free or paid, of a star; he could arrange within his company for the unusual casting of a popular play, or he could announce the first appearance of some novice performer likely to prove attractive. With diplomacy and luck, he might even combine two of these gambits.

In the 1770's and 1780's there seems to have been a custom (still prevalent in London on April 23, Shakespeare's birthday) of presenting a disconnected medley of scenes from Shakespeare, which allowed of the appearance at the same benefit of a number of leading players without the casting difficulties presented by a single play.[9]

When in 1789 Mrs Stephen Kemble, wife of the manager, took her benefit at Exeter, 'the performance concluded with a magnificent display of fireworks.'[10] This was, not unnaturally, considered rather dangerous, and was not repeated. But the idea seems to have been popular in the provinces, for 'A Grand Display of Fireworks' was included in a benefit at North Shields in 1791 without objection.[11] The performance of pantomimes at benefits was as a rule permitted only to Harlequin, Clown and Columbine, but the universally liked Fanny Kelly was allowed to have a pantomime *Harlequin Hoax* for her Drury Lane benefit in 1815,[12] and there was an earlier exception at Brighton when a certain Mrs Follett was allowed a pantomime at her benefit in 1795.[13]

Though leading players in a company expected quite humble requests before they would appear at the benefits of their juniors, the contractual obligations of the company in general included playing at one another's benefits, their salaries being covered by the charges of the night. But custom ordained, quite naturally, that a

[8] Harold Oswald, *op. cit.*, p. 38.
[9] John Adolphus, *op. cit.*, I, 68, 69.
[10] William Cotton, *op. cit.*, p. 7.
[11] Robert King, *op. cit.*, p. 31.
[12] Playbill in Garrick Club Collection.
[13] H. C. Porter, *op. cit.*, p. 19.

specific request, which could be refused, should be made to any performer if the studying of a new part were entailed.[14] The contractual nature of the benefit obligation was emphasized in 1836 when Alfred Bunn, manager of Drury Lane, desiring to spite his star Macready, 'exonerated' Cooper, the stage manager, from playing at Macready's benefit.[15]

Normally appearance at a benefit at another theatre required managerial permission in writing,[16] and even during the Summer closure, the Drury Lane contract of 1826 forbade appearance at any performance, benefit or otherwise, within six miles of the theatre.[17] For breach of this rule curious extremes of penalty are provided, for the offender 'shall forfeit one week's salary for every offence, and his or her engagement at the option of the manager.'[18]

When an artist desired to appear at a benefit outside his own theatre, he would normally approach his own management, but where several performers were concerned and the beneficiary was well known, a comprehensive permission might be asked for. Thus when Tom Dibdin, famous writer of light pieces and stage manager for forty-five years, took his last benefit at the Olympic in 1836, being then in very reduced circumstances, he had many friends in the profession who desired to help him, and he wrote to Alfred Bunn, manager of both Drury Lane and Covent Garden, asking for the release of those in the companies of the two theatres, naming some who had been with him during his management of the Surrey twenty years earlier. Bunn granted his request.[19]

When this same Alfred Bunn finally gave up the management of Drury Lane at the end of the season 1838-1839, he took a final benefit in March 1839. In his autobiography he prints a letter signed by his entire company requesting him to accept their services gratuitously on that occasion. Much derided as Bunn has been for his poor poetry, and with all his faults, this was a fine tribute, and all the more so as it is apparent that these artists had nothing to hope for from Bunn in the future.[20]

The memoirs contain some hair-raising stories of unscrupulous

[14] *Life of George Anne Bellamy*, IV, 125, 126.
[15] *Macready's Diaries*, I, 299.
[16] Thomas Leman Rede, *op. cit.*, pp. 76, 77.
[17] *Ibid.*, p. 72.
[18] *Ibid.*, pp. 76, 77.
[19] Alfred Bunn, *op. cit.*, II, 22, 23.
[20] *Ibid.*, III, 163, 164.

advantage taken of friendly, confiding benefit audiences. Not surprisingly, one of the worst is associated with the name of George Frederick Cooke. In 1791 Cooke was playing at Chester, and towards the end of the season he went with a party from his theatre to Liverpool, for the ostensible purpose of playing Mason's *Elfrida* for the benefit of Mrs Arnold.

> They suffered themselves to be advertised for the above piece, though conscious that they knew nothing of it, and had made no one preparation: the audience came as invited, and they without apology, or announcing any change of play, acted, or (as Cooke says, I doubt not with truth) murdered Thomson's *Tancred and Sigismunda*.[21]

No doubt it was this sort of thing that led to some announcements that cannot have been very encouraging to the box-office, such as the following in the "announce" bills of a rather unconfident beneficiary at Perth in 1805,

> he has selected the following Entertainments, under an assurance that their state of readiness and the promised assistance of his brother Performers, will enable him to present them perfect, so as to give satisfaction to that Public, whose patronage he solicits.[22]

Benefit audiences liked to receive not only their money's worth, but every attraction that had been advertised in the bill. At a benefit of Fitzball's at the Princess's in the 1840's, although Lola Montez had danced with a 'rapturous and universal . . . call for her reappearance,' yet a lady named Mrs Gratton had not arrived in time to sing a song for which she was set down, so 'the malcontents kicked up a bit of a row in the upper gallery.'[23]

There are a few more mixed examples of the endless scheming and ingenuity that were applied to the making up of a benefit bill, and these may best come under a general head.

A very lucky lady was Emily Soldene, a star in opéra bouffe in the 1870's and 1880's. In 1876 she played a season at the Park Theatre, Camden Town, and took a benefit there. 'For that night *Trial by Jury* was sent up from the Royalty. Rose Stella sang the Plaintiff

[21] William Dunlap, *op. cit.*, I, 48.

[22] Peter Baxter, *op. cit.*, Playbill opposite p. 32.

[23] Edward Fitzball, *Thirty-Five Years of A Dramatic Author's Life*, London, 1859, II, 95.

(originally played by Miss Nellie Bromley), Fred Sullivan was the Judge, and Mr Penley the Foreman of the Jury.' Emily Soldene had appeared quite often under the management of Richard D'Oyly Carte and seems to have been on good terms with him, but even so the transportation of an entire one-act comic opera to North London to give a second show at a benefit, when the company had already played once in their own theatre, is astonishing.[24]

When it could be secured, opera was always a very popular card to play, and now and again a benefit announcement in the provinces will give a shrewd idea of the general strength of the company concerned. When in 1846 Mr H. Deval, the musical director at New-castle, put up the opera of *La Sonnambula* for his benefit, it indicated that a good all-round vocal and histrionic stock company must have been assembled on Tyneside when the theatre had lifted up again from the very bad years of the early 1840's.[25] In order to obtain opera, it was considered justified to call in amateurs. Two artists taking a joint benefit at Norwich in 1839 were ambitious enough to produce Weber's opera *Der Freischütz* with the aid of local amateurs—'The Choruses will be numerously supported by the gentlemen of the Choral Society.'[26]

When the beneficiary put himself forward in a new character, he almost invariably selected one above and outside the level of his normal line of business, and sage advice was mostly disregarded when it came into conflict with the hope, not infrequently realized, of impressing his or her potentialities upon the manager. The following words, written about 1830, put the matter well from the woman's point of view.

> The benefit play of an actress is, at least, an opportunity of put-ting the town in possession of her own opinion of herself, and is, therefore, commonly seized for the purpose of extending the performer's claims. She can then invade the line of a rival, and correct the, perhaps, obstinate prejudice of a manager.[27]

There was a little more to it than putting the town in possession of an actress's own opinion of herself, for an actress or actor reach-ing some theatrical cross-roads, from age or other reason, could essay a contemplated new line of business at a benefit without too

---

[24] Emily Soldene, *op. cit.*, p. 189.
[25] Harold Oswald, *op. cit.*, p. 108.
[26] Bosworth, Harcourt, *op. cit.*, p. 31.
[27] James Boaden, *Life of Mrs Jordan*, I, 179.

binding a commitment. At the end of the season 1747-1748 Peg Woffington passed from Drury Lane to Covent Garden with the intention also of passing from comedy to tragedy, and, perhaps as a form of preparation, she took for her last benefit at Drury Lane the part of Jane Shore.[28] Another good example of this tendency is found in some episodes in the earlier career of Madame Vestris. After nine years as an opera singer who could also dance, and as yet unconscious that her future was to lie in leadership of the still unborn genre of extravaganza and burlesque, she had a period in which she seemed to attempt to open a line of retreat for herself into legitimate comedy, and for her benefits in 1824 and 1826 she essayed Mistress Ford in *The Merry Wives of Windsor* and Lady Teazle in *The School for Scandal.* Then she wavered back towards opera, and in 1830, the very year that was to inaugurate her triumphant lesseeship of the Olympic, at her benefit she sang in Meyer's *Romeo e Giulietta*, assisted by Madame Malibran.[29]

Tate Wilkinson, primarily a comedian and mimic, essayed Othello at his benefit in 1759, and came off well in the part.[30] Mrs Becky Wells at York in the later 18th century, having been denied a certain secondary part during the course of the season, put herself up in *Jane Shore* for her benefit, and so impressed that she was at once, somewhat ironically, given the part of Imogen.[31] Macready played Hamlet at the age of eighteen at his Newcastle benefit in 1812,[32] and again, for the first time in London, at his benefit nine years later.[33] Another bold proceeding of his was to present at his 1834 benefit *King Lear,* not in Nahum Tate's then customary perversion, but in Shakespeare's text.[34]

Six years after his sensational debut, Edmund Kean in 1820 tried at his benefit a new classic part, Jaffier in *Venice Preserved*, combining this with a sketch written to allow him to sing, dance, fence and give imitations, a novelty that drew £700 into Drury Lane.[35] Nearly eighty years earlier Garrick had shown that he too appreciated the value of contrast and versatility, when, on his Dublin

[28] Janet Camden Lucey, *op. cit.*, p. 140.
[29] Charles E. Pearce, *op. cit.*, pp. 95, 139, 156.
[30] Tate Wilkinson, *Memoirs of His Own Life*, I, 272-281.
[31] *Life of Mrs Sumbel, late Wells*, I, p. 53.
[32] W. C. Macready, *Reminiscences*, I, p. 48.
[33] *Ibid.*, I, 227.
[34] *Macready's Diaries*, I, 129.
[35] H. N. Hillebrand, *op. cit.*, p. 192.

benefit in 1742, he played a tragic and a comic character in *King Lear* and *The Lying Valet* in the same bill.[36]

Henry Irving, playing at Manchester in 1864, with only eight years' stage experience behind him, selected Hamlet for his benefit, which was the more audacious as Edwin Booth had played the part in that city only three years earlier.

A part that made considerable appeal to the younger 18th century player was Prince Hal. John Bannister played the part for his benefit in his first season on the stage in 1779,[37] and Thomas Snagg, taking a benefit, also at Manchester, in 1765, approached the matter with determination. 'I was resolved to shine, if at my own expense, and placed myself at the head of the bill—The Prince of Wales!—in *Henry the Fourth*.'[38]

But where a veteran had a famous character, it was usually and properly trotted out. When Corbet Ryder came to his farewell benefit at Perth in 1836, on his retirement from the stage, he can have had little doubt what part to play, for in his announcement that he would appear in *Rob Roy* he could add proudly, 'Performed by him upwards of 560 times in the principal Cities and Towns of Scotland.'[39]

Peg Woffington, whose impersonations in 'breeches parts' became renowned, played such a part in *The Female Officer* at her own first benefit at the Aungier Street Theatre, Dublin, in 1739.[40] Mrs Jordan first played the part of Sir Harry Wildair in *The Constant Couple* at her benefit in 1788.[41] This great comedienne also took the opportunity of a benefit in 1789 to make her first appearance as Rosalind, a part admirably suited to her comic genius. To the judgment of some 160 years later, it is astonishing to find that the performance 'somewhat divided the town, and the lovers of the sentimental and the humorous were arranged under the standards of Siddons and Jordan.'[42]

Versatility could also be an aim for actresses; Fanny Kelly at her Drury Lane benefit in 1817 played the lead in comedy, farce and

---

[36] Percy Fitzgerald, *Life of David Garrick*, I, 122, 123.
[37] John Adolphus, *op. cit.*, I, 42.
[38] Thomas Snagg, *op. cit.*, p. 24.
[39] Peter Baxter, *op. cit.*, p. 227.
[40] John Fyvie, *op. cit.*, p. 113, quoting Hitchcock's *Historical View of the Irish Stage*.
[41] James Boaden, *Life of Mrs Jordan*, I, 126.
[42] *Ibid.*, I, 139.

melodrama, throwing in her participation in "A New Medley for Six Harps".[43]

Benefit straws could show a young star how the wind of popularity was blowing, and at Covent Garden in 1819 Macready was gratified by many requests at the box-office that he should play Richard III for his benefit, though he did not yet feel himself ready for this trial.[44] This kind of audience interest might be pleasant enough, but if really strong views were expressed, the beneficiary had to give way for fear of riot. For his second Dublin benefit in 1742 Garrick first selected *The Fair Penitent,* but 'that play being disapproved of by several ladies and gentlemen', he substituted *Hamlet* for it.[45]

The choice of benefit play and part, so often leading on to fortune, could also mark a stage on the downward slope. A friend and rival provincial tragedian, writing of Charles Dillon at Wolverhampton about 1852, exclaims in sympathy,

> So dreadful was the state of affairs, that he was actually constrained to submit to the humiliation—I may say the ineffable degradation for a man of his genius—to have recourse to the ignoble expedient of enacting the hero of the Newgate Calendar drama of *Jack Sheppard* to fill the house at his benefit.[46]

There were also pitfalls and mistakes to be made. Dowton could consider himself unlucky when, for his benefit at the Haymarket in 1805, he selected for revival Foote's old comedy of *The Tailors,* and unwittingly precipitated a riot ending in the arrest of sixteen of the infuriated tailors of London, who considered themselves disparaged.[47] But Mrs Abington rather rushed upon her fate in 1786 when she opted to play the male low-comedy part of Scrub in *The Beaux Stratagem* at her benefit—for a wager, so it was said. This 'met with disapprobation', and she was considered to have disgraced herself.[48] Mrs Glover also made an unsuitable selection when she appeared as Hamlet for her benefit at Liverpool in 1821. She was told by a rather spiteful press that her best line was 'Oh! that this too too solid flesh would melt',[49] though in fairness it must be said

[43] Basil Francis, *op. cit.,* pp. 16, 17.
[44] W. C. Macready, *Reminiscences,* I, pp. 178, 179.
[45] Percy Fitzgerald, *Life of David Garrick,* I, 124.
[46] John Coleman, *op. cit.,* II, 631.
[47] R. B. Peake, *op. cit.,* II, 309.
[48] *Life of Mrs Abington,* p. 97.
[49] *Liverpool Theatrical Investigator,* I, 181, 195.

that she did better in the same part at her benefit at the Lyceum the following year, and was complimented by Edmund Kean.[50]

The limitations of tragedy or comedy were often disregarded at benefit time by performers who were not suited to play both—usually with dire results. John Bannister, an admirable light comedian, allowed himself both Richard III and Shylock in 1791 and 1795,[51] and Mrs Cibber chose Lady Townley in *The Provoked Husband* in 1744.[52] When Dowton, who was a low comedian, actually selected Shylock for his benefit in 1814, the year in which Edmund Kean had achieved undying fame in this character, it was an act of incredible folly,[53] but it must also have been a most fascinating attempt to put the clock back by more than seven years to the pre-Macklin era, when Shylock was habitually played as a low-comedy part in a red wig.

When in 1818 at Newcastle Joseph Grimaldi first played Bob Acres in *The Rivals,* and completed the evening with a pantomime, he probably fancied himself in Sheridan's comedy, for in the heyday of clownship good acting was as important as good knockabout.[54] But when, for his wife's benefit at Covent Garden in 1812, John Liston, the moon-faced comedian, played Romeo, he can but have been going for the burlesque laughs, and as he was given the regular strength and casting of the Covent Garden company in this play to support him, he must have nonplussed these worthies considerably.[55]

The case of Mrs Siddons, as it stands on the record, simply baffles modern judgment and must surely have given pained surprise even to contemporary judgment. This supreme tragic actress, whose Lady Macbeth froze the audience with horror, arrived at Drury Lane for the second time in 1782 aged twenty-seven and with three children. Her "line of business" was the tragic, and her indisputable qualities were those of majesty and matron dignity, qualities which intensified strongly with each year that passed. In her choice of benefit parts, it was very natural and human of her to select a role that gave a probability of reversing an earlier and unfavourable public judgment. In 1786, for her brother John Kemble's benefit at Drury Lane,

50 Walter Donaldson, *op. cit.*, pp. 137, 138.
51 John Adolphus, *op. cit.*, I, 270, 355.
52 John Fyvie, *op. cit.*, p. 77.
53 Walter Donaldson, *op. cit.*, p. 178.
54 Harold Oswald, *op. cit.*, p. 63.
55 Playbill in Garrick Club Collection.

Mrs Siddons 'was perhaps rejoiced to repeat the character of Portia in *The Merchant of Venice,* which had first introduced her to a London audience.' This is a polite understatement by her biographer, since that first introduction, under the management of Garrick, had been so little successful that it had sent her back into the provinces for nearly another ten years.[56] This rehabilitation was permissible, yet at one of her two benefits in 1785 she played Rosalind 'in a dress which more strongly reminded the spectator of the sex which she had laid down, than that which she had taken up.'[57] In other words, she was so prudish that she covered the breeches of the forest-bred youth with a ridiculous sort of abbreviated skirt. In the following year at her benefit she played Ophelia, which must have frightened the cast, especially the King, Queen and Laertes, a great deal. Next year this formidable woman played the gentle, timid Imogen at her benefit, and two years later in 1789, she crowned these benefit vagaries by appearing as Juliet. Even her sycophantic biographer Boaden admits that she 'was now in the "mid season of this mortal life"' — she was actually thirty-four — and 'the countenance was too strong for Juliet.'[58]

The assistance of a star would go far to ensure an overflowing benefit, and stars were, in consequence, sought after eagerly. At the very beginning of the 18th century, it was said of Mrs Oldfield that 'she refused to assist others in their benefits.'[59] There is some conflict of evidence about Garrick's practice, but the weight of this evidence is in his favour. Mrs Bellamy, who hated him, and is not reliable, says 'this is a favour he usually granted only to the first performers.'[60] Towards the end of his long career at Drury Lane, Garrick seems to have laid down the rule that he would play on the occasion of "farewell benefits" only, when the player concerned was taking leave of the stage.[61] Garrick's own statement, delivered in 1774, two years before his retirement, is 'I was long the slave of the

---

[56] James Boaden, *Life of Mrs Siddons,* II, 205.
[57] *Ibid.,* II, 166.
[58] *Ibid.,* II, 166, 206, 215, 279.
[59] John Williams (Anthony Pasquin), *op. cit.,* I, 219-224.
[60] *Life of George Anne Bellamy,* II, 110, 111.
[61] Garrick played at Mrs Clive's "farewell benefit" in 1769 (Percy Fitzgerald, *Life of Mrs Clive,* London, 1888, p. 81) and was tricked into playing at a similar benefit for Mrs Abington in 1776, but she failed to retire. (*Life of Mrs Abington,* pp. 81-84.)

stage. I played for every body's benefit, and even revived parts for them, and sometimes acted new ones.'[62]

There are at least three factual proofs of his assertion, for in 1756 Garrick gave his first performance of Lord Chalkstone in the final version of his own farce of *Lethe* for Mrs Clive's benefit,[63] and in 1768, for the benefit of John Palmer, he also provided novel casting by playing the Ghost in *Hamlet*.[64] In 1763 for Spranger Barry's benefit at Drury Lane, Garrick played Iago for the only time in his career.[65]

In spite of these examples, David Garrick proved a bad friend to the practice of stars playing at the benefits of their fellows, especially where a new part was concerned. In 1775 in an acrimonious correspondence with Mrs Yates, he laid down the rule that 'the managers would expect every performer to do for the house what they should do for the Benefits . . . why are not the proprietors to be profited by the performance of Mrs Yates in Almeria as well as Mr Cautherley?'[66]

This was something of a bombshell, for stars would clearly need to scrutinize more closely the parts they were prepared to enact in the friendly atmosphere of a benefit, if the playing of these parts could then be called for in the regular bill. Though managers seldom relinquished advantages they had obtained over players, this rule cannot have persisted very long after Garrick's retirement, for in the first quarter of the 19th century stars frequently appeared at benefits in parts they would not have dreamed of playing on other occasions.

Peg Woffington's Irish generosity came out in this matter, and 'not the lowest performer in the theatre did she refuse playing for.'[67] At Dublin in 1753, out of twenty-six benefits, she acted in twenty-four.[68]

Kean's benefit appearances were largely the result of generous impulses in which were mingled an element of harmless vanity. 'Many stories are told of his coming upon some wretched company

[62] *The Private Correspondence of David Garrick*, II, 65.
[63] Tate Wilkinson, *Memoirs of His Own Life*, III, 250, 251.
[64] Harold Child, 'Stage History of Hamlet', in New (Cambridge) Shakespeare ed. of *Hamlet*, Cambridge, 1934.
[65] Percy Fitzgerald, *Life of David Garrick*, II, 85.
[66] *The Private Correspondence of David Garrick*, II, 110.
[67] Tate Wilkinson, *Memoirs of His Own Life*, III, 206.
[68] Janet Camden Lucey, *op. cit.*, p. 181.

faced with disaster in some stolid town and pausing long enough to offer them a free benefit as Richard or Othello.'[69]

Managerial permission was needed for the appearance at a benefit of any artist outside the regular company of the theatre, but this was almost always accorded. The veto would, however, be invoked where the introduction of the outsider involved intentional offence. There was a case of this nature at North Shields in 1830 when a beneficiary arranged for the appearance as an actor at his benefit of the former manager of the theatre, with whom the then manager was on the worst possible terms: this was vetoed, amid an exchange of excited pomposities in the local press.[70] Newly risen stars were not allowed to play at benefits for their first season or two, their powers of attraction being then reserved for the manager's profit. G. F. Cooke writes of his first season in 1800 at Covent Garden, 'I was prevented acting for any of the benefits, Mr Lewis's excepted,' the exception in Lewis's favour being because he was stage-manager.[71] Nor did Edmund Kean play at any of the benefits during his first triumphant season of 1814-1815 at Drury Lane.[72]

An exception to this rule seems to have been provided by Mrs Siddons in her first season on her successful return to Drury Lane, for she was allowed to appear at the benefits of the four leading actors in tragedy, Smith, Palmer, Beasley and Brereton, also for the Theatrical Fund.[73] Mrs Siddons's visit to Dublin in 1784 was marred by a rather childish dispute about whether or not she should have played for the benefit of Digges and Brereton there. The matter pursued her back to London, resulting in the expressed displeasure of one Drury Lane audience, an explanation from the stage by the lady and exonerating letters by the gentlemen, though Brereton's was rather sour in tone.[74]

A minor piece of etiquette was that stars could never be invited to play in afterpieces. Macready foamed at the mouth when asked to do so in 1836 for a 'wretched creature' he particularly disliked.[75] But, for all his indignation, he had played *Rob Roy* as an afterpiece

[69] H. N. Hillebrand, *op. cit.*, p. 197.
[70] Robert King, *op. cit.*, p. 66.
[71] William Dunlap, *op. cit.*, I, 141.
[72] Playbills in Garrick Club Collection.
[73] James Boaden, *Life of Mrs Siddons*, II, 11, 12.
[74] *Ibid*, II, 98-100, 106-113, 115-118.
[75] *Macready's Diaries*, I, 292, 299.

at his own benefit at Drury Lane in 1825 and *William Tell* at Bristol
in 1836.[76]

Relationship was, on the usual "thicker than water" principles, an
outstandingly good claim to benefit assistance, though very liable to
cause jealousy, especially in the provinces. Though stardom lay
thirteen years in the future, the benefit value of relationship emerges
from a playbill of one of Edmund Kean's appearances as a child
actor in 1801 at the Great Room in Store Street, Bloomsbury, which
is described with literal truth as being 'for the benefit of his
Mother.'[77] But twenty-seven years later the benefit relationships in
the Kean family had changed greatly. There were two main causes
of estrangement between the great Edmund Kean and his son.
Charles had taken the side of his wronged though unsympathetic
mother in the break-up of Edmund's marriage, and Charles had
gone on the stage against his father's wishes, though he had been
sent to Eton to qualify himself for some more highly regarded
calling. There was a reconciliation of sorts in 1828, when both played
together in Howard Payne's *Brutus*, which has a father and son
aspect in its story, for Charles's benefit at Glasgow, but as the
atmosphere must have been electric, it is not surprising that there
are two distinct accounts of the affair. The official account,
emanating in 1859 from Charle's Kean's biographer, indicates a full
reconciliation, and adds the story of the father teaching the son a
lesson in the emotional control needed in the "impersonation" of
acting by whispering in his ear at a dramatic moment, 'Charley, we
are doing the trick.' The unofficial account comes from the man
who was Master Carpenter and general factotum at the Theatre
Royal, Glasgow at that time, and he tells a different story. According
to this, and it rings true, Seymour the Glasgow manager tricked
Edmund Kean into playing a night in Glasgow on his way through
to his cottage in Bute without letting him know that Charles would
be playing, still less that it was his benefit,

> and Kean never knew that such was the case until he came into
> the theatre to dress and saw the bill. The old man got into a
> thundering passion upon making the discovery, and wanted to
> leave the house; but his friend Jerry Cunningham, who was
> with him, urged him to go on . . . except when on the stage

[76] Alfred Bunn, *op. cit.*, II, 30, 31.
[77] Playbill described in p. 6 of Ifan Kyrle Fletcher's catalogue No. 1 of 1938.

together, father and son never met or recognized one another previous to the fall of the curtain.[78]

Between the years 1813 and 1819, that is to say after her retirement from the stage, Mrs Siddons acted on nineteen occasions and always without personal profit. Three of these performances were for the benevolent purposes of the theatrical funds, and two at the express desire of the Princess Charlotte in 1816. Against these five non-family appearances, ten were for the advantage of the family of her dead son in Edinburgh, and four were for the benefit of her brother Charles Kemble and his wife.[79]

In the constant animosities and feuds of the players, there even came moments when policy or malice dictated the absence of a star at a benefit. In 1748 Macklin was again a member of the Drury Lane company, though unreconciled with Garrick from their former quarrels. His gesture of spite at his benefit was to ask the services of every member of the company except Garrick, leaving the inference to be drawn that he disdained such aid.[80]

Stars were notoriously unreliable, and freer of promise than performance, a fault that will be dealt with later, but the ever-enterprising Tate Wilkinson put an extremely bold front on Foote's refusal to implement his promise of performing in 1759 by playing himself the part intended for the star, who had also been his master in mimicry, and mimicking Foote throughout.[81] Since Foote had also denied the use of the play, this was in addition an instance of unauthorized performance at a benefit in days when no law of copyright restrained such proceedings.

The hazards of a star at your benefit might well, in the deep-drinking days, include the possibility of his having given offence by his last appearance or perhaps non-appearance, and being required by the audience to do penance. In the season 1802-1803 at Covent Garden, that incorrigible toper G. F. Cooke had, through one of his prolonged drinking bouts, been unable to play in a new play called *The Harper's Daughter*, for which he had been announced. His next appearance was in *King John* "on Mrs Litchfield's night", and he was in consequence hissed on his first entrance and had to address the house before he obtained their absolution.[82]

---

[78] John Cole, *op. cit.*, I, 163, 164, and Malcolm Mackintosh, *op. cit*, p. 223.
[79] *Ibid.*, I, 34.
[80] Percy Fitzgerald, *Life of David Garrick*, I, 225.
[81] Tate Wilkinson, *Memoirs of His Own Life*, I, 272-280.
[82] William Dunlap, *op. cit.*, I, 250.

Though stars would play gratuitously for "small people", the leading performers would have to pay, or at least offer to pay, though hoping the star would be magnanimous enough to refuse the offer. Tom Sheridan, who was both manager and star at Dublin in the 1760's, 'gets £30 for playing at any of the actors' benefits.'[83] This was a high figure, for Edmund Kean only asked twenty guineas, which he then usually remitted.[84]

This hope that the star would remit his fee at a benefit went down the whole heirarchy of the stage, and the whining Everard is shown in a better light than usual when he writes of a season in Edinburgh 'As I had danced, gratis, twice for my friends, so I did the third and last time for the benefit of the door-keepers, although they offered me two guineas.'[85]

Offers for the services of stars at provincial benefits varied, and two received by Cooke in 1802, both of which he refused, were, to share the house with the beneficiary after expenses at Brighton, and to play at Richmond for £10.[86]

When the benefit was that of the manager, he was prepared, if necessary, to pay well for his star, especially in the provinces. Elliston, whose very poor season at Manchester in 1810 had been redeemed only by a triumphant visit from Mrs Jordan, offered her £50 to return and play for his benefit.[87] Macready paid Braham twenty guineas to sing at his benefit in 1834, and tried unavailingly to engage Paganini as well.[88] But as an undertone to all such negotiations was the desperate desire of the beneficiary to obtain a star of some sort at any price, and when an eccentric character such as Anthony Le Brun, Prompter at Margate in 1803, is concerned, this comes out plump. He writes to Cooke

> Now, Sir, if you would condescend to perform for me here, on my benefit-night, that will effectually fill the house, and whatever part of the night's profits you shall please to take, I shall cheerfully give it, and be thankful to you for your kindness.[89]

Right at the other end of the Thespian scale, an outside star was

[83] Recollections of the Life of John O'Keeffe, I, 323.
[84] George Raymond, op. cit., p. 332.
[85] E. C. Everard, op. cit., p. 129.
[86] William Dunlap, op. cit., I, 213.
[87] A. Aspinall, op. cit., p. 127.
[88] Macready's Diaries, I, 133.
[89] William Dunlap, op. cit., I, 254.

still a star, and had to be paid. Mrs Charke tells of a queer, shabby little benefit at the Tennis Court, some time in the early 1730's, at which she was asked to star and offered a crown. She held out for a guinea, plus the use of white stockings and a clean shirt, obtaining all three in the end.[90]

By 1825 it had become established that the manager cast the pieces to be played at benefits, though it was generally allowed as a matter of courtesy that the beneficiary should choose the part he wished to represent.

Unusual casting of a favourite piece could be relied upon to pay benefit dividends, and here the smaller players might sometimes derive advantage from the ambitions, however ill-conceived, of their betters. The ballad-opera singer Mrs Becky Wells once assured a good benefit for a colleague by her appearance in the Siddonian part of Lady Randolph in Home's tragedy of *Douglas*.[1] But it was possible that novel casting might be of greater service to the artist so cast than to the beneficiary. Elizabeth Farren had come out in London at the Haymarket in 1777, but had made no particular impression until, at Parson's urgent representations, she played Lady Townley in *The Provoked Husband* at his benefit in the following year and achieved a triumph.[2]

Under the heading of novel casting, or at least a novel idea, would come one more of Mrs Bellamy's numerous devices, casually mentioned by her in the words 'For my benefit this season, I had the farce of *The Oracle,* acted by Lilliputians,' i.e. by a cast of child actors.[3] Another believer in novelty was an actor Richard Jones, who for his benefit at Covent Garden in 1815, 'amongst other attractions, introduced a masquerade on the stage,'[4] for which George Colman the Younger wrote a prologue. The benefit of De Camp the Newcastle manager in 1828 ended with a still more remarkable masquerade, when those intending to come in character or dominoes were invited to choose their dresses at the theatre 'which, so far as the wardrobe goes, will be at their service.'

[90] *A Narrative of the Life of Mrs Charlotte Charke*, p. 87.

[1] *Life of Mrs Sumbel, late Wells*, I, 93, quoting 'Chronicle'.
[2] John Fyvie, *op. cit.*, p. 266.
[3] *Life of George Anne Bellamy*, II, 169.
[4] R. B. Peake, *op. cit.*, II, 352.

Original casting at benefits was not always disinterested; it could represent managerial kite-flying. Garrick tried the part of Sir Harry Wildair in *The Constant Couple* for Peg Woffington's benefit in 1743, but as this proved a failure, he relinquished the part to the lady again.[5] The element of managerial experiment was also present in 1822 when Kean played Osmond in the old play of *The Castle Spectre* for the benefit of Russell, the stage-manager of Drury Lane.[6] This experiment succeeded, and the play was put into the regular bill before the end of the season.

Into the same class of kite-flying would come the reappearance at a benefit of a former favourite anxious to return to the boards after a period of withdrawal for whatever reason; if the old charms were shown in public to be undiminished, an engagement for the following season would follow. An example of this is Mrs Baddeley's playing, after a two years' absence, for Miss Younge's benefit in 1773, which led to a re-engagement by Garrick.[7]

The principle of putting one's best foot foremost at one's benefit was constant to all ranks of the profession. When the scene painter attached to the Newcastle Theatre, took his benefit in 1827, this was the proper occasion for the unfolding of a new work from his brush, an act drop of 'A view of Newcastle and Gateshead taken from St Ann's Rope Walk.'[8]

A novelty of artistic demerit which nevertheless attracted the curious, consisted in the reversal of roles. As one instance of this, in 1836 at the Garrick Theatre in Whitechapel, where the manager Benjamin Conquest was a low comedian, there was a reversal of roles at his benefit, he playing William Tell, while the tragedian of the company, Freer, played Jerry Sneak in Foote's comedy of *The Mayor of Garratt*.[9] Though this kind of casting was a favourite benefit attraction at one time, it was not without its dangers if the casting was of a burlesque nature and the audience failed to see the joke. Thus when at Paul Bedford's farewell benefit at the Queen's in 1868, some scenes from *Othello* were included with Sothern as Othello in Dundreary whiskers and Buckstone, a low comedian, burlesquing Iago, while the other characters played their parts straight, 'the joke at first produced some signs of disapprobation

[5] Percy Fitzgerald, *Life of David Garrick*, I, 127.
[6] H. N. Hillebrand, *op. cit.*, p. 255.
[7] John Fyvie, *op. cit.*, p. 251.
[8] Harold Oswald, *op. cit.*, p. 75.
[9] Frances Fleetwood, *op. cit.*, p. 45.

from the audience', but Sothern stepped forward and said that it was done for a benefit, and that if he and Mr Buckstone had been asked to turn somersaults they would have tried to do so, even at the risk of breaking their necks. Mr Buckstone said at the end of a scene that if he and Mr Sothern had made fools of themselves, it was only to benefit a brother actor.[10]

A new play at a benefit was a proposition with several very distinct sides to it. On the one and upper hand, it was a famous compliment for a dramatist to pay to a star who was an especial friend. 'Mr Foote presented Mr Macklin with his spick span new farce of *The Englishman in Paris* for his benefit'—this was in 1752.[11] Garrick paid the compliment twice, with the final version of his farce of *Lethe* for Mrs Clive's benefit in 1756,[12] and with *Bon Ton* for Tom King's in 1775, though in this case the edge of the compliment was blunted by the farce being announced as by an anonymous author.[13] Another lucky beneficiary was Clinch, for whose benefit at Covent Garden in that same year of 1775 Sheridan wrote his short farce, *St Patrick's Day; or The Scheming Lieutenant*.[14]

On the other hand, even though benefit audiences were very tolerant, and in the early 19th century prepared to meet opposition with cries of 'Turn out them geese!' should hissing be heard,[15] yet if a new play were "damned", this was in a measure a reflection upon the beneficiary. But for all that, between about the years 1780 and 1810 the production of lesser new farces and musical afterpieces at performer's benefits happened constantly at both Patent Theatres with varying success. But as so many of these were poor in quality, by 1820 we find the expression "a benefit farce" used as a term of contempt.[16] There are records of considerable boldness by players in backing their own judgment of a play. Michael Kelly, who believed in Prince Hoare's musical play, *No Song, No Supper*, afterwards so successful, insisted in getting it up for his benefit at Drury

[10] Clement Scott and Cecil Howard, *op. cit.*, II, 360. and note.
[11] Tate Wilkinson, *Memoirs of His Own Life*, I, 256.
[12] *Ibid.*, III. 250-251.
[13] R. B. Peake, *op. cit.*, I, 333.
[14] Allardyce Nicoll, *Late XVIIIth Century Drama 1750-1800*, Cambridge, 2nd ed., 1952, p. 185.
[15] Thomas Dibdin, *op. cit.*, I, 119.
[16] Miss Benger, *Memoirs of Mr John Tobin*, London, 1820, pp. 100, 101.

Lane in 1790, although it had already been refused by the management,[17] and Mrs Becky Wells a year earlier produced *The Dramatist*
by Frederick Reynolds under similar circumstances.[18] Prince Hoare
seems to have been a believer in the launching of his plays at
benefits, for he pursued this course with one tragedy and two lighter
pieces in addition to *No Song, No Supper*.[19] O'Keeffe's best known
play, *Wild Oats,* also appeared at a benefit,[20] and was at once taken
over by Covent Garden. O'Keeffe actually went one better about
1778 when he contrived what might be called a collective benefit
play for the Portsmouth company. He adapted one of his old
sketches to the topical conditions of the place 'and, free from any
self advantage, had it performed for the benefits of Wheeler, Booth,
Mattocks and Mrs Kennedy.'[21] Fortunate indeed was the artist who
could not only cajole a new play for a benefit out of a successful
author, but get it tailored to measure. An extreme case of this
occurred in 1831 at the Olympic when Mrs Glover, the popular
actress of old-women parts, secured for her benefit 'a neatly-
constructed two-act drama, by the popular author, Mr Wm Leman
Rede, called *Woman's Revenge* and written expressly for the benefi-
ciaire and her family, by whom all the characters were sustained—
the performers being Mrs Glover, her daughters Mrs Evans, Mrs
Bland and Miss Mary Glover, her son Edmund, and her son in law
Mr Bland.' The occasion was a "bumper" and the old theatre held
£20 more than its reputed money capacity.[22]

The boldest of all were those who produced pieces of their own
composition. Mrs Clive was one; she brought out a farce of her own,
The Rehearsal; or, Bays in Petticoats, at her benefit in 1750. Though
both she and Garrick played in it, the piece was "damned".[23]
Undeterred, she produced several other farces of her own at her
later benefits, that of 1763 being above the level of such entertainments.[24] Others to have their plays "damned" at their own benefits,
both in 1799, were King and Miss de Camp, though the actor had

[17] S. M. Ellis, *op. cit.,* pp. 174, 175.
[18] *Life of Mrs Sumbel, late Wells*, I, 125.
[19] John Adolphus, *op. cit.,* I, pp. 252, 322, and James Boaden, *Life of Mrs Jordan*, I, 299.
[20] *Recollections of the Life of John O'Keeffe*, II, 152.
[21] *Ibid.,* I, 373.
[22] Malcolm Mackintosh (The Old Stager), *op. cit.,* p. 76.
[23] John Fyvie, *op. cit.,* p. 84.
[24] *Ibid.,* p. 87.

the excuse that his play had been written thirty years earlier.[25] Tom Dibdin was really in rather a different category as he was more of a dramatist than an actor. He had better luck when he put up a piece of his own, *The Jew and the Doctor*, for his benefit at Maidstone in 1798, as a political case at the Assizes had brought down many important lawyers from London, with the result that his play was at once recommended to Covent Garden.[26] The ranks of the successful benefit actor-authors included Elliston, with a melodrama *Rugantino; or, the Venetian Outlaw* in 1805,[27] James Anderson with an adaptation from Schiller in 1846,[28] John Philip Kemble with his classic tragedy *Belisarius* (Hull in 1778 and York in 1789), and Edmund Kean, who when at Waterford in 1810, produced at his benefit a melodrama of his own writing, *The Cottage Foundling; or, the Robbers of Ancona*, apparently with success.[29]

In the provinces a new play by a local author was always a very good card. When Edmund Kean was playing with Andrew Cherry's company in South Wales in 1810, he produced for his benefit a new piece, *Zaffine; or, The Knight of the Bloody Cross*, written by the poetess Anna of Swansea, who was a sister of Mrs Siddons and all the Kembles.

But at certain provincial theatres in the 18th century, Norwich for one, no new plays were allowed at benefits.

An unusual complaint by the players, apparently peculiar to Thomas Harris's management of Covent Garden at the end of the 18th century, was that he claimed the right to take over as his property, without further payment to the author, any new play produced at a benefit at his theatre.[30] This complaint is hardly borne out by the course of Tom Dibdin's dealings with Harris over new plays at benefits at about the same time as the players' complaint, which was 1800. Of one Dibdin says, 'Mr Lewis did me the favour to ask a comedy from me for his benefit; I say "favour", because he stipulated that in case of success the theatre should pay for the play, which Mr Harris confirmed.'[31]

[25] John Adolphus, *op. cit.*, II, 44.
[26] Thomas Dibdin, *op. cit.*, I, 212.
[27] George Raymond, *op. cit.*, p. 111.
[28] James R. Anderson, *op. cit.*, p. 139.
[29] Giles Playfair, *Kean*, London, 1939, pp. 62, 63.
[30] *A Statement of the Differences subsisting between the Proprietors and Performers of the Theatre Royal Covent Garden, given in the Correspondence which has passed between them.* pp. 38, 39.
[31] Thomas Dibdin, *op. cit.*, I, 362.

This is an early case of one of those short options that managers still take on plays produced on special occasions—nowadays Sunday night performances. Harris took up his option with most gratifying promptitude by saying to the author as the final curtain fell, 'Dibdin, you may ask the treasurer for £300; two for the play, and one for the copyright.'[32] Mrs Jordan produced at her benefit in 1790 the farce of *The Spoil'd Child*, containing the character of Little Pickle, which enjoyed sixty years of success at least,[33] but a similar essay two years later with *The Village Coquette* was not so successful, 'the management not choosing to adopt it.'[34]

First appearances fell into two categories, one that, if not purely catchpenny, drew its main attraction from the name and parentage of the beginner, the other a sincere encouragement of budding talent.

The first appearance about 1728 of Mrs Charlotte Charke, Colley Cibber's eccentric daughter, fell into the first category. 'Mrs Thurmond's [benefit] coming on soon, who understood that I was designed for the Stage the Season following requested that I Might make my first appearance on her Night.'[35] No doubt Mrs Thurmond reaped her harvest from playgoers who wished to be among the first to inspect the powerful manager's daughter.

Charles Macklin was extremely proud of *his* daughter, and on the occasion already mentioned when Foote presented him with a 'spick span new farce for his benefit', the dramatist went further and allowed for paternal feelings, as 'the character of Lucinda was drawn on purpose to introduce Miss Macklin to advantage . . . Her dancing and music master were purposely introduced to prove her various excellencies.'[36]

At Drury Lane in the season 1744-1745, Peg Woffington, at the very height of her fame, did not appear at her own benefit in order that it might be devoted to the purpose of launching her younger sister Polly (Mary). The girl played Cherry, the excellent chambermaid part in *The Beaux Stratagem*, but Peg had to endure the

[32] *Ibid.*, I, 364.
[33] James Boaden, *Life of Mrs Jordan*, I, 175.
[34] *Ibid.*, I, 214.
[35] *A Narrative of the Life of Mrs Charlotte Charke*, p. 48.
[36] Tate Wilkinson, *Memoirs of His Own Life*, I, 256.

humiliation of seeing her sister make an uncompromising failure.[37] This girl afterwards married Captain Hon. Robert Cholmondeley, a marriage which gave rise to Peg's celebrated retort to the irate father: 'My lord, I have much more reason to be offended at it than your lordship, for whereas I had before but one beggar to support, I have now two.'

A variation to the bringing forward at benefit performances of sons and daughters, and one that was sure to please, was when a young wife made her first appearance at her husband's benefit. This was the case at the King's Theatre in 1815 when Madame Vestris, destined for forty years of fame and a special place in stage history as the first actress-manageress, came out in the principal part of Proserpina in von Winter's opera *Il Ratto di Proserpina* at the benefit of her first husband Armand Vestris.[38] There is a certain pathos in the coincidence that Madame Vestris also made her last appearance for the benefit of her second husband, Charles Mathews the Younger, at the Lyceum in 1854. She had reached the end of her journey, and with bankruptcy immediately impending, she rose from a sickbed to play the leading part in a play with the ironic title of *Smiling Through the Clouds*.

At least the element of sympathetic notoriety was attached to the curious affair at Birmingham about 1765 when Yates, the manager there, desirous of helping a friend, Mrs Davies, whose husband had recently gone mad, urged her to go on the stage and launched her as Indiana in *The Conscious Lovers* at a free benefit. Not unnaturally, the wretched woman was seized with stage fright and unable to utter a single word.[39]

The encouragement of budding talent shall be represented by a good-natured action on Mrs Bellamy's part.

> When my benefit came to be fixed, the manager and myself had some words relative to Miss Wordley's performing on the occasion. That young lady wished to try her fortune upon the London stage. I desired much to oblige her; as I was at this time so attached to her, that I feared she would be obliged to enter into some country company, or go to Ireland, if she could not get an engagement in town.[40]

[37] Janet Camden Lucey, *op. cit.*, p. 103.
[38] Charles E. Pearce, *op. cit.*, pp. 13, 301.
[39] John Fyvie, *op. cit.*, p. 316.
[40] *Life of George Anne Bellamy*, IV, 58, 59.

All the same, though George Anne Bellamy had been quite prepared to have some words with the manager relative to Miss Wordley, when the night came, the star played Juliet as usual, and the protegée was brought out in the afterpiece.

Mrs Bellamy made her own first appearance at Covent Garden as Miss Prue in *Love for Love* at the benefit of an actor named Bridge-water in 1742, when she would only have been fifteen years of age, and though it is probably correct to say that even so clever a débutante would scarcely have been given so good a part at that age except at a benefit, the credit must be divided between the actor and shrewd old John Rich the manager, to whom the girl had already received an introduction, for she had powerful connections as the natural daughter of Lord Tyrawley.[41]

The next case, that in which, 'one evening over our bottle', Ned Shuter invited Tate Wilkinson to play, at his benefit at Covent Garden, a part in a farce of Garrick's normally played by Woodward at Drury Lane, reveals, in addition to the encouragement of a promising novice, another benefit practice in which only the boldest could indulge—that of purloining for the night a piece that was the property of the rival Patent Theatre.[42] A bribe to the prompter would usually procure a copy of the script, but the enterprise seems foolhardy for both Garrick and Woodward were at their artistic zenith, where Shuter and a clever novice protegé would be no match for them. Wilkinson felt this and protested that his part 'was certainly the most improper character for me in the whole round of the drama'—but he played it nonetheless.

This helping of novices at benefits lasted right into the middle of the 19th century. In 1852 John Coleman, a robustious provincial tragedian, taking a benefit at Ipswich in *Monte Cristo,* added *Sylvester Daggerwood,* a vehicle for imitations, to the bill 'to enable an aspiring amateur, who came to me with an introduction, to make his first appearance on the stage.'[43] That aspiring amateur was J. L. Toole, one of the most famous of comedians of the next forty years. Actually Toole had had a curious brief appearance prior to that, when he was taken behind the scenes at a benefit night at the old Pavilion in the East End, and a turn having failed to arrive, he

[41] John Genest, *op. cit.,* IV, pp. 8, 9. *The Oxford Companion to the Theatre* gives the date of Mrs Bellamy's first appearance as 'possibly 1744'.
[42] Tate Wilkinson, *Memoirs of His Own Life,* I, 97.
[43] John Coleman, *op. cit.,* II, 560.

was urged to substitute and almost pushed onto the stage to do so.[44]

Yet even in this matter of first appearances at benefits, managers often tried to extract some advantage for themselves. Girls were sent on at benefits in small parts with the promise of an engagement if they acquitted themselves well. One such to attain afterwards some position was Mrs Waylett, who started in this fashion 'at the Bath theatre, where she appeared on the 16th of March 1816 as Elvina in *The Blind Boy*. The character is of no importance . . . but our heroine's appearance made the effort interesting. This was for Mrs Chatterley's benefit, and she was engaged in consequence.'[45]

This business of a trial part at a benefit could have its sorrowful side if the understanding on the matter were not a truly clear one. Edward Everard played a short part in Miss Farren's benefit at the Haymarket in 1779.

> Mr Colman, sen. condescended to come round and speak to me, and desired me to leave my name with Mr Jewell; this was considered as an engagement, and after hearing Mr Colman's words in the Green-room respecting me, Mr Bannister, Mr Aicken, and others, wished me joy, and congratulated me.[46]

But he was not engaged at the Haymarket after all, and it nearly broke his heart.

The opportunities afforded by benefits began to be seized upon by stage-struck amateurs in the last quarter of the 18th century. Prior to about 1830 such appearances were not commercialized as they later became, but only took place either if the theatrical beneficiary perceived some solid advantage to himself, or if the appearance were virtually forced upon him by higher, usually managerial, interest. One example of each class is given below. In 1771 Powell's benefit at York brought £115, 'which sum has seldom been exceeded at common prices.' The reason was the first appearance of 'a young gentleman of York city, whose name was Banks . . . well educated and heir to a good fortune.'[47] The other side is represented by an example forty-five years later. Tom Dibdin[48] was experienced in all branches of the theatre, and can hardly have appreciated the arrangement he was called upon to make when he was joint

[44] John Hatton, *op. cit.*, p. 87.
[45] *Amatory Biography of Mrs Waylett*, p. 2.
[46] E. C. Everard, *op. cit.*, p. 100.
[47] Tate Wilkinson, *The Wandering Patentee*, I, 91.
[48] Thomas Dibdin, *op. cit.*, II, 91.

manager of Drury Lane under a Committee in 1816. 'On the night
of my benefit . . . a young lady of the name of Murray, introduced
by a member of the committee, made her début as Cecilia in *The
Chapter of Accidents*: she was well received and repeated the
character, but was not engaged.' In the provinces these amateurs
seem to have become sometimes a definite nuisance, and the Committee of the Theatre Royal, Norwich ordered, at the end of the
18th century, that a certain Captain Pye was not to be allowed to
appear at any benefit.[49]

[49] Minute Books of the Theatre Royal, Norwich, Vol. 1.

XII—THE BILLING

THE BENEFICIARY'S FIRST ACTION to advertise his or her "night" was the preparation and wide distribution of a preliminary bill, known as an "announce bill", setting forth the nature of the social patronage, the intended glories of the evening, and the various places where tickets could be obtained.

A dilemma arose at once, for while the benefit had to be represented in a most attractive light, if stars were announced and failed to appear, the disappointment of the audience might become vocal. Tate Wilkinson, on the occasion in 1759 when Foote let him down so badly, congratulated himself that he had been wise enough not to bill the star's name until he had received confirmation.[1] Farren in 1833, losing his head, was mad enough to announce Macready's name before asking him. The tragedian stigmatized this as 'the base conduct of Mr Farren, who, it seems, in aggravation of his impertinence in advertising my name for his benefit without my leave, contrived to have me paragraphed in the newspapers.'

He then asked his diary 'Qu. What shall I do with the contemptible blackguard?', and answered himself 'I am almost ashamed to be angry with such a reptile.'[2]

Stars who promised their services and then backed out could usually do so with impunity, unless they met a lady as determined as Miss Falkner proved to be at Covent Garden in 1751. Spranger Barry had let her down in this manner, but the lady then 'continued his name in the bill to the very last, in spite of repeated forbiddances . . . On the night of performance she went on before the play, and read a prose address to the audience . . . recounting the story.'[3]

It was always most distressing when the harmony of a benefit night was disturbed by one of those perennial theatre disputes about the relative size and position in the bill of artists' names. At Drury Lane in 1769, Mrs Clive seemed to be fortunate when Garrick agreed to appear for her farewell benefit in the new character of Lord Chalkstone he had recently added to his farce of *Lethe*, but the

---

[1] Tate Wilkinson, *Memoirs of His Own Life*, I, pp. 272-281.
[2] *Macready's Diaries*, I, 42.
[3] Tate Wilkinson, *The Wandering Patentee*, I, 22-27.

omission of her name from the first announcement of this led to an unhappy squabble.[4]

The "announce bill" and the subsequent bill of the benefit night itself required the approving initial of the manager before they could be printed. This proviso was not only customary, but included in the Rules of some theatres. At Drury Lane in 1826 'any one who sends an advertisement to a public print, or issues a bill, unless signed by the acting manager, shall forfeit one week's salary.'[5]

At the Marylebone Theatre in 1837 the ungrammatical rule provided for the forfeiture of engagement of

> any person . . . introducing any matter whatever . . . without the Manager's permission first had and obtained, and for which purpose two copies of such bill must be brought, one for the Printer and the other for the manager to file, who will then sanction or disapprove, and sign them for publication.[6]

Though the necessity for the approval of the manager was absolute, yet the amount and method of payment for billing in benefit "charges" seems to have varied a great deal. At the major London and provincial theatres, the benefit "charges" included the normal advertising for a stock night, the beneficiary paying for such extra advertising as he might require, though visiting stars in the provinces were not normally consulted about these extras, and were often appalled at the amount of additional payments under this heading for which they were held responsible. Lesser members of provincial stock companies sometimes received the advantage of normal managerial advertising on their "night", at other times and places they found that the advertisement of a benefit was expected to be drawn, sent, and paid for, by the performer himself—though, of course, after the manager's approval.

The Spectator in 1712, desiring to help a certain actor with a "puff" for his benefit, inserted the following.

> The haughty George Powell hopes all the good natured part of the town will favour him whom they applauded in Alexander, Timon, Lear, and Orestes, with their company this night, when he hazards all his heroic glory in the humble condition of honest Jack Falstaff.[7]

[4] Percy Fitzgerald, *Life of David Garrick*, II, 344.
[5] Thomas Leman Rede, *op. cit.*, pp. 76, 77.
[6] Copy in the Collection of the late Malcolm Morley.
[7] John Doran, *op. cit.*, p. 397.

Managerial control of announcements must have been lax in the early days to allow of Spiller at Lincoln's Inn Fields in 1719 advertising a performance as 'for the benefit of himself and creditors.' Theophilus Cibber, though he was a first rank comedian at the time, was just as candid. In 1746 he appealed thus to the consideration of the public:

> As I have, in justice to my creditors, assigned over so much of my salary as reduces the remainder to a very small pittance, I very much depend on the indulgence and encouragement of the town at my benefit, whose favours shall be gratefully remembered, by their very humble servant, — Theophilus Cibber.[8]

Primitive advertising devices that would now be regarded as puerile, were resorted to, and proved effective. In Dublin in 1764 Wilson drew attention to his benefit by having the advertisement of it in the newspaper printed upside down. Pleased with this piece of ingenuity, he said 'And without this hum, perhaps my advertisement might not have been noticed.'[9] The actual printing of advance benefit bills and advertisements in the newspapers was supplemented by any other publicity devices considered likely to help to attract an audience, and devices that had become outworn in London twenty years earlier or more could still pack a provincial theatre. So at Newcastle in February 1845, when at the end of the pantomime Mr J. Wood the Clown took his benefit, he revived for the astonishment of his simple patrons an old publicity stunt of Usher the Clown at the Coburg, and announced that as a great treat and the greatest feat ever witnessed in Newcastle, he would sail in the character of Clown from the King's Meadows to Newcastle Bridge at three o'clock in a washing tub drawn by four geese,[10] a great feat that one imagines to have been influenced more by the current of the River Tyne than by the geese.

Yet, curiously enough, as emerged during a lawsuit in 1862, this managerial 'permission first had and obtained' did not exonerate the beneficiary from his legal liability for the contents of his benefit bill. Benjamin Webster, in dispute with a newspaper, printed a libel on its proprietor as a standing heading to the Adelphi playbill for a whole week. But Toole's Benefit falling during the week, he

---

[8] *Ibid.*, pp. 397, 398.
[9] *Recollections of the Life of John O'Keeffe*, I, 59.
[10] Harold Oswald, *op. cit.*, p. 105.

requested the removal of the paragraph from his benefit bill, and thereby, but only thereby, escaped from being joined as a party to the subsequent suit.[11]

[11] *Theatre Notebook*, Vol. 4, No. 3, p. 58.

FROM THE ACCOUNTS OF THE ELIZABETHAN STAGE such as that in Dekker's *The Gull's Horn-book,* it is clear that noblemen and gentlemen had then enjoyed the privilege of bringing their stools onto the area of the stage itself, while in the Restoration period Pepys's diary shows that gallants had ready access behind the scenes. By the beginning of the 18th century the practice had acquired a curious conventional extension upon benefit nights known as a "building on the stage", or simply "building". The playbill would announce 'for the better accommodation of the ladies, the stage will be formed into an amphitheatre, where servants will be allowed to keep places.'[1] We have a description of what this amphitheatre consisted of from an actor writing long after Garrick had swept the whole thing away in 1762.

> Suppose an audience behind the curtain up to the clouds, with persons of a menial cast on the ground, beaux or no beaux crowding the only entrance . . . The stage spectators were not content with piling on raised seats, till there [sic] heads reached the theatrical cloudings; which seats were closed in with dirty worn out scenery . . . but when that amphitheatre was filled, there would be a group of ill-dressed lads and persons sitting on the stage in front, three or four rows deep.[2]

In 1709 this seems to have excited the admiration of Steele, for in the first number of *The Tatler* describing Betterton's farewell night, he wrote 'There has not been known so great a concourse of persons of distinction; the stage itself was covered with gentlemen and ladies, and when the curtain was drawn, there appeared also a very splendid audience.'[3]

Yet it was not long before "building" was recognized to be 'the greatest nuisance that ever prevailed over an entertainment for the elegant and general resort of any metropolis.' Tate Wilkinson paints the ridiculous picture when

Romeo was breaking open the supposed tomb, which was no

[1] Tate Wilkinson, *Memoirs of His Own Life,* III, 160, 161.
[2] *Ibid.,* III, 160-162, 164, 165.
[3] Robert W. Lowe, *Life of Thomas Betterton,* London, 1891, p. 179.

more than a screen on those nights set up, and Mrs Cibber prostrating herself on an old couch, covered with black cloth, as the tomb of the Capulets, with at least (on a great benefit night) two hundred persons behind her, which formed the background, as an unfrequented hallowed place of *chapless* skulls, which was to convey the idea of where the heads of all her buried ancestors were packed.[4]

The stage boxes at the side were also "built out" with two or three rows of seats in front of them, and when in a piece a conventional gallant had to escape from a balcony or scale one, he was forced to push his way through with many apologies.[5] Mrs Bellamy tells of being accosted rudely by a drunken man as she was trying to go on.[6] These annoyances and absurdities were not likely to increase respect for players or playhouse, as most of the persons on the stage cared nothing for illusion, only desiring to see the actors and actresses at close range. But the main supporters of "building" were the incommoded players themselves, inconvenience and sometimes insult being justified by the addition of perhaps a hundred pounds to their benefit profits from the secondary audience upon the stage.

"Building" was not universal at benefits, for when managerial anticipation considered that the auditorium itself would suffice for the audience to be expected, the bill would carry the words 'N.B. Not any building on the stage.'[7] This was a nice calculation sometimes falsified by a beneficiary's optimism, and there were cases at Drury Lane in both 1746 and 1756 of building on the stage for crowds that failed to materialize, the dispiriting remedy being 'to shut in the benches with a flat scene.'[8]

It needed a manager of Garrick's standing to carry through the abolition of "building", and even so some delayed resentment over this decision may have contributed to foment the rioting he encountered in the following year. Yet Garrick and his then partner Lacy were most careful to afford a *quid pro quo* to the players, who were the main supporters of the "building" system. Davies, Garrick's first biographer, deals with this important point.

The comedians, by losing the advantage of an amphitheatre

[4] Tate Wilkinson, *Memoirs of His Own Life*, III, 161, 162.
[5] Percy Fitzgerald, *Life of David Garrick*, II, 22-24.
[6] *Life of George Anne Bellamy*, II, 137.
[7] Tate Wilkinson, *Memoirs of His Own Life*, III, 160, 161.
[8] *David Garrick Private Correspondence*, I, 46, and Tate Wilkinson, *Memoirs of His Own Life*, III, 222.

on a benefit night, would be considerable losers; and to remedy that evil, Mr Garrick very judiciously observed, the plan of reformation, must be preceded by a considerable enlargement of the playhouse; and if it could be so contrived, that the space before the curtain might contain as many persons as had formerly filled the pit, boxes, galleries, and the stage, no body would have any pretence to murmur.[9]

Garrick's attitude had, however, been assisted by the continuous rise in favour of pantomimes from 1717, for the complicated machinery needed for these entertainments had already resulted, for reasons of safety, in a prohibition of all visitors behind the scenes on pantomime nights, thus undermining the supposed rights of the nobility and gentry.

In Ireland Thomas Sheridan, the Manager of the Smock Alley Theatre in Dublin, had succeeded in abating this nuisance as early as the years 1745 and 1746 at the cost of some rioting and with the aid of two strokes of luck.

The first of these was that the Viceroy, Lord Chesterfield, was in his box when

> Young St Leger, being heated with wine, and stirred by Miss Bellamy's beauty, kissed the back of her neck as she passed him in full sight of the audience; whereupon in a second she turned and smacked him full in the face. At this the Lord Lieutenant rose in his box and heartily clapped his hands, an example the audience was not slow to follow.[10]

Next season there was another grave riot in January 1746-1747, and fortunately for Sheridan, the ringleader, Kelly of Galway, who was drunk, behaved abominably, for 'climbing over the spikes, he got upon the stage, and very soon made his way to the green room, where . . . he addressed Mrs Dyer in gross and indecent terms', afterwards withdrawing to the pit to pelt Sheridan on the stage with oranges. This outrage provoked a reaction, and

> Several citizens advanced in years, who were seldom seen at a theatre, were so sensible of the advantages and importance of a well regulated stage, that they declared to Mr Sheridan and his friends, that they would now more than ever, appear there, and

[9] Thomas Davies, *op. cit.*, I, 332.
[10] J. Fitzgerald Molloy, *The Romance of the Irish Stage*, London, 1897, I, 191.

doubted not being able to protect the manager, and the actors in general in the discharge of their duty.[11]

Under the protection of these grave seniors, Sheridan was able to clear his stage of idle and frequently drunken spectators.

In England there is one reference to suggest that Bath had preceded Drury Lane by seven years in banishing benefit audiences from the stage itself. The *Bath Journal* of January 27, 1755, contains an announcement,

> The great demand for box places having obliged Mr Brown to lay the pit and boxes together, rather than crowd the stage, and impede the performance — He flatters himself the Town will so far indulge him, as to accept the first gallery as pit, which shall be kept entirely for that purpose, and the upper gallery at eighteen-pence.[12]

But all theatrical customs, the bad ones included, die very hard, and about 1770 at Sheffield, Lee Lewes complained not only of spectators on the stage, but actually in a pantomime, a thing that had not been known for twenty years and more in London. He was playing Harlequin on his benefit night, when

> the scenes being so overcrowded on that night by those who could not get into the front of the house, that many stood on the stage, and, at the moment I was going to take my leap, I perceived a woman standing directly in the place through which I was to escape.[13]

The result was an accident in which Lewes was badly concussed.

There were spectators on the stage during Elliston's "break-in" benefit at the Opera House in 1804,[14] dealt with in the next chapter, but these were merely the occupants of the boxes, involuntary refugees from their own seats from which they had been ejected by the mob.*

---

* On special occasions spectators were to be seen on the London stage several times in the 19th century: for instance at Banti's benefit at the King's Theatre, Haymarket, in 1802; at Grimaldi's farewell in 1828; and in 1840 at the visit of Queen Victoria and Prince Albert to Covent Garden, when *The Times* reported (February 29) 'a party of visitors, perhaps more numerous than there generally are on such occasions'—significant words. V.C.C-B.

[11] Robert Hitchcock, *An Historical View of the Irish Stage from the earliest period down to the close of the season 1788*, Dublin, 1788, II, 171-180.

[12] S. Penley, *op. cit.*, p. 39.

[13] Charles Lee Lewes, *op. cit.*, I, 66-68.

[14] James Boaden, *Life of Mrs Jordan*, I, 161, 162.

As with many another custom, the lingering on of this one was more protracted in the provinces. Perhaps the most excusable such affair was that at Charles Kean's benefit at Glasgow in 1828 when his father Edmund came up and played for him, and it is related with gusto in the memoirs of the then Master Carpenter of the theatre.

Seymour (manager of the Theatre Royal) had rightly calculated upon such a cast being a draw. The house was one of the largest, if not the very largest, I ever saw in the glorious Old Royal. Upstairs and down the crush was the same; and so, when the audience portion of the house could positively hold no more, Seymour resolved to stow them away whereever there was a "coigne of 'vantage" behind, at a charge of three shillings each. By his order, I was made "first robber" for this department, at the stage-door, where, I assure the reader, I took fully £40— which at the rate mentioned per head, shows that over 250 persons were on this memorable evening accommodated behind the scenes. The word "scenes" reminds me, by the way, that on this occasion there was no change of scene. There could not be, in fact, owing to the intrusion of so many of the public, and the piece was literally performed from beginning to end in a circle on the centre of the stage . . . After the tragedy the bulk of the audience left, and those who had been behind the scenes were sent to the front, where there was now plenty of room for them to witness the after-piece.[15]

Even on humbler provincial stages there was building of a sort. About 1800 Masterman's company played a miserable public house at Haverfordwest in Wales and expected at highest receipts of no more than nine pounds. Yet the benefits ranged from twenty to thirty-two pounds.

In order to account for this, I must observe that our scenes were entirely taken down, seats borrowed from inns or Assembly Room . . . stage so filled that it was difficult to get on even by entreaty . . . Many persons paid who never heard a line of the play nor cared about it. They were well contented below, with sending for bottle after bottle for the company.[16]

[15] Malcolm Mackintosh (The Old Stager), *op. cit.*, p. 223.
[16] Cecil Price, *op. cit.*, pp. 90, 91.

Perth provides three still later cases of spectators on the stage and in the wings. At John Wilson's benefit in 1835 some of the public stood in the wings and behind the scenes. At Ryder's benefit in 1838, 'the space behind the stage was so crowded as to interfere with the movements of the actors and actresses.' The same applied to Miss Smith's benefit in 1840. This seems to have been tolerated with a kind of misplaced pride in its being a tribute to the artist concerned.[17]

The astonishing final flicker of the Elizabethan heritage of stools on the stage seems to have taken place at Nottingham in 1856, when at James Anderson's "farewell night" (i.e. his benefit) the audience was so large

> that the gentlemen of the orchestra were compelled to quit their seats and play behind the scenes . . . Ladies and gentlemen paid to be allowed to go behind the curtain and stand all night between the wings . . . The actors were perfectly astonished at being mixed up with the audience, and all declared they had never witnessed such a sight before.[18]

At benefits the public was prepared to accept enhanced prices for a long and strengthened entertainment, and even the subscribers' Silver Tickets did not admit on benefit nights.[19] But this rule seems sometimes to have been waived to the players' disadvantage, for it was one of the complaints at Covent Garden in 1800 that the management possessed a normally exercised right to introduce orders on an actor's benefit night. This was merely one included in a string of grievances; there was no direct suggestion that the management abused the right, and indeed it would be to the advantage of the beneficiary to be seen by other managers and those in the managerial orbit likely to represent or be in touch with prospects of advancement; but the system was felt with some justice to be inequitable on the actor's one night of the season.[20]

At Birmingham in the 1820's the theatre rules provided that there should be no alteration in prices at benefits. This was probably exceptional, but perhaps the Birmingham manager wished to be

[17] Peter Baxter, *op. cit.*, pp. 242, 253, 269.
[18] James R. Anderson, *op. cit.*, p. 232.
[19] S. Penley, *op. cit.*, p. 25.
[20] *A Statement of the Differences subsisting between the Proprietors and Performers of the Theatre Royal Covent Garden, given in the Correspondence which has passed between them*, p. 65.

certain of avoiding the occasional disturbance brought about by benefit price increases.

In general the admission at half price after nine o'clock did not apply to benefits when "Nothing under full price taken" became the rule. Then came the question of "laying into the boxes" the whole or some part of the pit, for which operation the expressions "added and railed in at box prices", "put together" and "taken into" were also used.[21] The point was that the pit so "laid" was charged at the higher price of a box seat. But the law of swings and round-abouts balancing out seems to have applied from early days in the entertainment world, and Mrs Cibber writes to Garrick in 1746 of her brother Tom Arne, 'he is forced to put his pit and boxes together, which I reckon will be no advantage to him, ladies' hoops taking up more room than the difference in price.'[22]

Upon great occasions such as Garrick's first benefit at Goodman's Fields in 1742 and Mrs Clive's farewell benefit at Drury Lane in 1769, all the pit was laid into the boxes,[23] but by the 19th century, possibly owing to the protests of regular pit patrons, the custom, at least in the Patent Theatres, seemed to be declining. In 1801 Mrs Jordan wrote of her benefit at Drury Lane 'They want me to lay part of the Pit into Boxes—but it cannot be allowed.'[24]

The number of rows of pit laid into the boxes at a benefit was a matter as proudly announced as the gross receipts, especially perhaps in the provinces. At their respective benefits at Drury Lane in the season 1744-1745 Garrick had five rows of the pit railed off, and Peg Woffington six.[25] When Miss Farren went to play for her sister's benefit in Yorkshire in 1787, three rows of pit were laid into the boxes,[26] and seven rows were scored by Tate Wilkinson at Dublin in 1758[27] and by Mrs Jordan at Leeds in 1786.[28] Mr Brown at Bath in 1755 laid the whole of his pit into boxes, and so did Mrs Siddons at her benefit there in 1781, though equally 'reserving the front rows of the gallery for the gentlemen of the pit.'[29] About 1795 at Swansea Miss Lascelles "from Covent Garden" took a benefit, of which was

[21] Tate Wilkinson, *Memoirs of His Own Life*, I, 172, 173.
[22] *The Private Correspondence of David Garrick*, I, 40, 41.
[23] Percy Fitzgerald, *Life of David Garrick*, I, 95. John Fyvie, *op. cit.*, p. 96
[24] A. Aspinall, *op. cit.*, p. 45.
[25] Janet Camden Lucey, *op. cit.*, p. 93.
[26] John Fyvie, *op. cit.*, p. 261.
[27] Tate Wilkinson, *Memoirs of His Own Life*, I, 172, 173.
[28] John Fyvie, *op. cit.*, p. 363.
[29] S. Penley, *op. cit.*, p. 59.

written 'a greater benefit was never known at this theatre; the whole of the pit was converted into boxes.'[30] But when Elliston also threw the pit into the boxes at Bath in 1792, he made the mistake not so uncommon with him, of giving the screw one extra turn with 'the gallery advanced to pit price'—the gallery here meaning presumably the upper as well as the first circle—so the result was a disturbance calling for one of his most Ellistonian oleagenous addresses to the audience before peace was restored.[31]

Though the motive for the "laying together" of pit and boxes came from the beneficiary, probably after consultation with the manager and the box-book keeper if the wisdom of the step was in doubt, there is one case, very flattering to the lady concerned, where the initiative came directly from the audience. This was the benefit of Miss Grimani (afterwards Mrs Charles Young) at Bath about 1802 or 1803, when

> a deputation of influential residents waited on the manager of the theatre with a request that he would allow the whole pit and orchestra to be converted into stalls, that her receipts might be the larger. The sum netted in consequence—private presents included, was 500 l.[32]

A comical-pathetical example of the Thespian urge to show a bold front to rival, larger establishments, even in the matter of seating, comes from an announce bill that has been preserved of a benefit performance at the old theatre in East Grinstead in 1758. 'On account of the prodigious demand for places, part of the stable will be laid into the boxes on one side, and the granary open for the same purpose, on the other. Vivat Rex.'[33]

The actual practical method by which this laying together of pit and boxes was effected, is not altogether clear. In Georgian theatres the pit had a single entrance, which would have made difficult a distribution of pittites into those in the railed off portion and those in the seats at normal prices, if all had entered the pit together. Dr Richard Southern thinks that, in some theatres at least, the box fronts and partitions on the lower tier may have been removable, so that the pit patrons paying box prices reached their railed off pit

[30] Cecil Price, *op. cit.*, p. 85.
[31] George Raymond, *op. cit.*, p. 92.
[32] Julian C. Young, *op. cit.*, I, 31.
[33] James Boaden, *Life of Mrs Siddons*, I, 15, 16.

seats through the boxes rather than from the pit itself.[34] Something analogous can be seen to this day at the Theatre Royal, Bristol, built in 1766, where the present main entrance to the stalls is down a few steps from the circle (the old box tier), a box front having been removed at some time or another.

One other variation in benefit prices may be noted, for at Wilkinson's benefit at Portsmouth in 1758, instead of the pit being laid into boxes, 'by desire the gallery and pit all made one price.'[35]

At provincial theatres the benefit season would call for some furbishing up of the house and its approaches. A Manchester benefit bill of 1766 includes the assurances 'The way will be swept to the Theatre, and the house illuminated with wax. N.B. It will be MOONLIGHT.'[36] Less mud on the players' shoes and stockings, and relief for one night from the offensive smell of tallow candles. Even smaller, though not unimportant details were provided for, and this is another from East Grinstead in 1758. 'N.B. The great yard-dog, that made so much noise on Thursday night, during the last act of *King Richard the Third*, will be sent to a neighbour's over the way.'[37] Even more important than any vocal accompaniment by the yard-dog to Bosworth Field was personal security, so the beneficiary saw to the inclusion in his benefit bill at North Shields in 1781 of the comforting words 'that Captain Bover and Lieut. Oakes of the Press Gang had given their word of Honour that no seamen would be interrupted by them from 4 p.m. until 12 p.m.'[38]

Finally a glimpse of the house that the beneficiary and his entire family had prayed for during twelve months. 'At three o'clock, all the avenues to the theatre were completely stopped up, carriages could not approach the doors, and the ladies were obliged to go from the stage over the spikes of the stage box to their places in the side boxes.'[39]

[34] *Oxford Companion to the Theatre* (s.v. Auditorium), Oxford, 1951, and letter to the Writer.
[35] Tate Wilkinson, *Memoirs of His Own Life*, I, 195, 196.
[36] John Williams (Anthony Pasquin), *op. cit.*, I, 146, 151.
[37] James Boaden, *Life of Mrs Siddons*, I, 15, 16.
[38] Robert King, *op. cit.*, p. 18.
[39] John Williams (Anthony Pasquin), *op. cit.*, I, 313.

XIV—THE SETTLEMENT

A REASONABLE PRELIMINARY to the financial settlement following a benefit was for the beneficiary to make arrangements to ensure that the money expected was duly taken at the doors and handed over to the theatre Treasurer. At major London theatres and at reputable provincial theatres, the management would be vigilant, the money-takers of integrity and in adequate strength, so such precautions would hardly be needed. But if, for any reason, an artist was taking a benefit at a theatre other than that in which he was normally engaged, or appearing in certain provincial theatres, particularly Dublin, he seems to have been regarded as fair game, and even his utmost precautions would scarcely avail. The King's Theatre, or Opera House, seems to have had an especially bad reputation in this respect. In 1804 Elliston took a benefit there, at which there was a "break-in", as it seems to have been called, the entrances being stormed by the pit and gallery crowd and the money-takers thrust aside or beaten down.[1] Elliston harangued the audience in his most typical manner of making the best of a bad job, and said that

> convinced as he was, every person honouring him with their presence meant to pay, he begged leave to observe that the deficiencies would be received on the following morning at his house, No 6, Great Russell Street, Covent Garden.[2]

But as a more directly practical measure, he also 'sent his play-wardens among them with pewter plates, to collect the unpaid dues; and something was recovered.'[3]

The amount recovered is conjectural, and though one authority puts it as high as £600, this seems unlikely, even allowing for those 'who had been forced in without the option of disbursement.'[4] The same thing happened there to Michael Kelly the singer, and he claimed that, though the house was crammed, the money return was only £25.[5]

---

[1] R. B. Peake, op. cit., II, 308.
[2] George Raymond, op. cit., 105, 106.
[3] James Boaden, Life of Mrs Jordan, I, 161, 162.
[4] John Cole, op. cit., I, 82.
[5] S. M. Ellis, op. cit., p. 335.

At the Haymarket in the 1790's—but this was out of season, when nobody cared much about casual benefits—it could be just as bad. Here is the wail of the unfortunate Everard.

> I wanted to provide my own money-takers and door-keepers, but this could not be; I was obliged to have those commonly belonging to the theatre, though I engaged to pay them their usual stipend to stay at home and keep out of the way; — as I expected I was most shamefully robbed. I had in the same house the week before, played . . . for the benefit of a Mr Walker; he declared, that my house appeared better and fuller than his; — his amount was L120, and mine not quite L55.[6]

Leman Rede's advice to the novice included a warning that every performer who takes a benefit has a right to put his own cheque-takers at the door, and that no false notion of delicacy should prevent an actor taking this precaution.

Of the proceedings at Dublin in 1811 the nervy and irritable Charles Mathews sent home a terrifying account to his wife.

> I was told that I must have two friends at every door, or the plunder would be horrible. These friends I obtained, but . . . hundreds passed the check-takers without delivering them [sic], numbers without paying at all; others with tickets in their pockets who could not deliver them. One of my friends at the door was beaten and bruised, his pocket picked, and over-powered.[7]

In humbler provincial spheres than Dublin the same thing might occur, and Everard had a "break-in" at his benefit at Windsor in in the 1790's, the crowd rushing the doors at four o'clock.

> . . . the crowd was so great and pressing that they threatened to break down the doors if they were not opened—they rushed in like a torrent—no one there so soon as to take money—what could I do? no getting them out: I was forced to rely upon their own justice and generosity, and from my putting an advertisement in the paper, many had the honour to step forward; but on a moderate estimate, I suppose the house at last was twelve pounds deficient.[8]

[6] E. C. Everard, *op. cit.*, pp. 151, 152.
[7] Mrs Mathews, *op. cit.*, II, 146, 147.
[8] E. C. Everard, *op. cit.*, p. 138.

An echo of this ramp comes in another memoir heart-cry from Ashton-under-Lyne about 1830. 'My benefit . . . Seventeen pounds five shillings was received at the doors—goodness knows how much more! Neville being money-taker, without checks or account books.'[9]

But such events were exceptional at the better theatres, and the principal cause of friction between artist and manager at a benefit settlement almost always arose from an attempt either to withhold some part of the receipts, or to impose additional "charges" beyond the fixed sum agreed as the normal charges of the night. It should be understood that, in addition to the fixed "charges" of the house (varying from £40 to £240 according to period and theatre), about which there could be no great argument at the settlement, there were certain other deductions made, of the reasonableness of which the two parties to the settlement might take different views. The least arguable was the charge for Supernumeraries, for they were always paid upon a nightly basis, their numbers could be checked upon the stage, and their rate of pay was fairly uniform. If special music was required, there must be a payment to the leader of the band for its arrangement. Properties had to be purchased for any piece not in the normal theatre repertoire; the property-master submitted an itemized list, but there could be items added later. Finally there was the account for extra printing and advertising; the businesslike beneficiary, particularly if a touring star, would agree this account with the manager before the work was put in hand, but such artists were in a small minority. There seems to have been a good deal of trouble over settlements in Liverpool in 1821. Apparently Vandenhoff's "charge" of £60 was run up to £100, though he chose for his benefit *Brutus,* which had been played the whole season. A few years earlier Grimaldi, when visiting at Liverpool, had been presented with eleven extra bills amounting to £34 for "extra properties, etc, etc", when he put his foot down and refused to receive any more.[10]

At Drury Lane a deduction was made from benefit profits for the Theatrical Fund established by Garrick,[11] but this may have been

[9] Edward Stirling, *op. cit.,* I, 83, 84.

[10] *Liverpool Theatrical Investigator,* I, 485. This little theatrical newspaper, which consistently attacked the Liverpool managers, is a most biased authority, but it is evidence for the nature of minor abuses at a provincial benefit settlement, whether or not anything of the sort could be proved at Liverpool.

[11] *The Private Correspondence of David Garrick,* I, 630.

merely the most painless method of extracting the beneficiary's annual subscription. There were some curious little financial snobberies that at times affected the benefit receipts and the subsequent settlement. At Edinburgh in 1780, Mr Bailey, a member of Tate Wilkinson's company, on taking his benefit advertised 'At the end of the third act half price will be taken.' Wilkinson relates that this was resented by the audience 'as mean and an affront . . . after the third act not one person entered the doors', and in general the benefit was a failure.[12]

As the Stage was the only licit profession except millinery in which a woman could earn her own living, there was one aspect of benefit settlements, the husband's power over his wife's money, which is no longer present in our minds. When Garrick insisted that Mrs Baddeley should leave a Dr Hayes with whom she was living, she tried to make it a condition of compliance that her salary should be paid weekly into her own hands, but her husband objected on the ground that he still remained liable for her debts.[13] "Perdita" Robinson later complained that her husband's creditors became so clamorous that the whole of the receipts from her benefits had to be handed over to them.[14] There were three even worse cases. When Drury Lane treasury ignored a formal notice from Glover to pay the bulk of Mrs Glover's salary to him, he sued the theatre management with success.[15] Mrs Cibber was actually forced off the stage for a couple of years after 1738 until the rascally Theophilus Cibber could be prevailed upon to come to a legal agreement that would restore to her the control of her own earnings.[16] Mrs Billington wrote to her mother from Dublin, probably in 1783, 'Billington came the morning after my benefit, and striped me of every bit of cloaths, and about seventy pounds in money' though she did not mention the provocation she had given her husband by the flagrancy of her affair with the manager, Daly.[17]

When two lesser artists took a joint or "double" benefit, the law or custom seemed to be that, in the absence of any prior arrangement, the entire takings, doors and tickets, were divided equally, and a settlement of this nature led to anomalies and surprised hard-

---

[12] Tate Wilkinson, *The Wandering Patentee*, II, 94, 95.
[13] John Fyvie, *op. cit.*, p. 235.
[14] *Ibid.*, p. 292.
[15] *Ibid.*, p. 291.
[16] *Ibid.*, p. 70.
[17] *Memoirs of Mrs Billington*, p. 65.

luck stories. That kindly mentor of the beginner, Leman Rede, put the point best.

> If you take half of the house with any other performer, it will be necessary to have a private agreement with regard to tickets; for if he can only sell ten, and you fifty pounds' worth, it would be manifestly unjust that the tickets should be equally divided. The best way in these cases, is to divide the money taken at the doors equally, and for each party to stand by his own tickets.

Tom King ran into a delicate situation on the settlement of his benefit, when starring in Dublin in 1766. His benefit was a clear one, which meant, of course, that the night's charges, including salaries, would be paid by the manager. But at that time salaries were being paid considerably in arrear in Dublin, so there was muttering among the company that the English star should be able to take the proceeds of his clear benefit away with him, while they had to wait. This came to King's ears, and on the night of the benefit, before the curtain rose, he entered the green room in his stage costume with a large purse of guineas in his hand, and 'going round the room, asked them one by one what might be the amount of their salary by the night. Each answered; and on the answer, he drew from his purse, and presented it to each in turn.' The actors then became ashamed, and all but one refused to take the money.[18]

Frederick Reynolds, when a young dramatist in the 1780's, writes of his first benefit, 'As soon as the play was over . . . I rushed into the treasury, to learn the extent of my profits,'[19] and found that they were £8. Though an author enjoyed a time advantage over a performer in point of rushing to the treasury, most junior benefieciaries were probably on the threshold of that office when it opened the following morning. Seniors behaved more circumspectly. Richard Cumberland did not draw his profits of the author's night of *The West Indian* in 1771 as they accrued. He waited until 'Mr Evans the Treasurer came to my house in Queen-Anne-Street in a hackney coach with a huge bag of money, he spread it all in gold upon my table and seemed to contemplate it with a kind of ecstasy.'[20]

It seems probable that the Treasurer in his hackney coach would

---

[18] *Recollections of the Life of John O'Keeffe*, I, 151.
[19] Frederick Reynolds, *op. cit.*, I, 323.
[20] *Memoirs of Richard Cumberland*, London, 1807, I, 297.

also take their benefit profits to leading players, for banker's drafts were little used, though there is some mention in memoirs of bank-notes of large denominations generally used by wicked noblemen intent upon seduction. Indeed it is more than probable that the Treasurer was assiduous in such visits, for he seems to have received a tip, 'the customary fee' Cumberland calls it, for his services.

In the early days of the touring system—this instance is of about 1868—the very payment of salaries was irregular, to say the least of it, and the announcement of a benefit, as so often, a mere excuse to attract another five or ten pounds into the house. 'I had a "benefit" at Cheltenham. The Assembly Rooms were crammed, and all the chairs for a mile round pressed into the service, but I did not touch a red cent,'[21] wrote Emily Soldene thirty years later.

In smaller provincial towns methods of settlement were much more direct. George Vandenhoff relates (though his story is not actually of a benefit) that when he was playing a few nights at Blackburn in 1840 on 'a clear half of the receipts', the unlettered Lancashire manager came to his dressing room at curtain fall with bulging pockets, and tipped upon the table a £5 note, two sovereigns and £22 in silver and copper. The two men sat down there and then to divide this in silence into equal halves. Then there was a stiff allowance of brandy 'for luck', and the actor comments, 'I am inclined to think, that though it was not the most formal, or "high-Roman fashion" of settlement, it was, perhaps the fairest and honestest that I have ever been favoured with.'[22]

A typical instance of a not uncommon form of settlement is recorded by Edward Stirling of a time about 1843 when he was playing at Sheffield in the company of the father of Tom Robertson the dramatist. After his benefit, he was invited to supper by the Robertsons; later the others slipped away, leaving him alone with the pretty Mrs Robertson, a baby in her arms. She pleaded to be allowed to send the money after him the next week, when her husband had taken his own benefit, as they were in difficulties. Stirling consented and never got his money.[23]

Another minor injustice was inherent in the system. While the deduction of the manager's charges was constant, the gross amount accruing to the beneficiary before deductions had one illusory fac-

[21] Emily Soldene, *op. cit.*, p. 60.
[22] George Vandenhoff, *op. cit.*, pp. 104, 105.
[23] Edward Stirling, *op cit.*, I, 142, 143.

tor. That portion of the receipts represented by the public paying its money at the doors would be in the Treasury all right, but the larger portion always came from the sale of tickets by the performer to his friends and acquaintances. The tickets thus issued were reckoned by the Treasurer as part of the gross receipts, but it was not always so easy for the poor player to obtain what was due to him, while undue pressure for payment might alienate the whole of a powerful family or some other local circle of influence. The solid majority of benefit playgoers no doubt handed over their money as they received their tickets, but the two other classes, those who had not the money on them and those who asked to be put down for a number of tickets and then omitted to appear, seems to have been distressingly numerous. In addition the beneficiary would be expected to produce a certain number of free admissions for such important personages in his life as his landlady and the principal tradesmen who had become creditors during the earlier part of the season. When the Covent Garden management in 1800 supported an increased benefit charge by arguments based upon the receipts of a number of benefits, the angry actors brought these matters forward, telling the manager roundly that he was

> without having any *datum* in your possession from which you are enabled to form a judgment of what is a Benefit receipt, being entirely ignorant of what Tickets are given away, and what sold, and of the deficiency in the payment for Tickets, which every Actor is liable to experience.[24]

Everard has afforded an instance of an aggrieved beneficiary trying to make the audience into the jury on a benefit squabble on the subject of a benefit date. There is an even remoter case in 1834 at Perth where an actor named Hudspeth during his benefit 'attempted to agitate the people in the gallery' against the manager Burroughs about an amount of £2-18-0, alleged still to be owing from the actor's benefit in Dundee, the previous town visited. The Perth gallery did not consider this to concern them, and declined to be agitated.[25]

It was not always the manager who was the one to behave badly. In 1837 an actor, before joining the Bristol company, took a benefit

[24] *A Statement of the Differences subsisting between the Proprietors and Performers of the Theatre Royal Covent Garden, given in the Correspondence which has passed between them*, p. 58.
[25] Peter Baxter, *op. cit.*, p. 216.

at the Haymarket. 'Yet this Mr Stevens not only did not pay the Actors, Band, Bills, etc, but absolutely insulted many persons who had neglected their own business to attend to his.'[26]

As a difficulty usually arose in the manager's obtaining his due repayment of the charges from the performer should the benefit prove to be a losing one, by the beginning of the 19th century the necessary safeguards were no longer left to custom but were given sanction by their inclusion in the normal form of contract used at the theatre. Stephen Price's contract for Drury Lane during his lesseeship in 1826 took the form of stating the clauses relating to benefits with the proviso that the sum of two hundred guineas benefit charges 'exclusive of extra charges for new dresses, copying, printing, advertising, and supernumeraries, if any there be', was payable to the treasurer in advance, so that the consequent safeguards had legal standing as agreed penalties for the non-performance of the main clause calling for payment of the charges in advance. The safeguards were the right to retain the first two hundred guineas taken at the doors, deduction from the weekly salary, responsibility of the executors and the estate in case of death, and the giving of reasonable security if demanded.[27]

In the provinces the benefit was sometimes a moment for a rather grim reckoning with the manager, represented in the memoirs of the unlucky Everard in the form of the following dialogue dating from the 1790's.

'Well, Mr Cooper, I'm glad to see you; you are now the last person I have to settle with; let's proceed to business. The half of your ticket money to me is L2 10s, and two guineas I lent you on your arrival here, making together L4 12s due to me. I suppose you can now discharge it?' 'Indeed, sir, I am sorry to say that I cannot; I have not five shillings in the world.' 'Fie for shame, sir; very pretty, sir; and I suppose you owe money in the town too?'[28]

The wording of this little speech also indicates the exact way in which the manager, before the American Stephen Price thought of the clause in the contract just mentioned, safeguarded his charges, for with the receipts being made up of the cash taken at the doors

[26] *Figaro in London*, April, 1837.
[27] Leman Rede, *op. cit.*, p. 70.
[28] E. C. Everard, *op. cit.*, p. 125.

and the tickets sold by the beneficiary, the manager 'took as his share all the cash and a proportion of the ticket money', which evidently represented the night's expenses or charge.[29]

But the manager could be generous as well as exacting when the artist was loyal and reliable, and at Norwich in the 1770's an artist was made an advance of £50 on account of his benefit. Doubtless this was no exceptional case.[30]

The last solicitude of a well-mannered actor who had taken a final benefit on leaving a provincial town was to insert "A Card in the press". That of Mr Raynor at North Shields in 1816 said that, if he ever returned to the town, 'the humble abilities which they had been pleased to notice in so distinguished a manner shall be studiously exerted to merit their approbation.'[31]

It may have been possible that some general acknowledgement in the press was called for, even though the beneficiary were not leaving the town, at least in the first half of the 18th century, for Tate Wilkinson quotes from a pamphlet *The Case of Thomas Kerrigan*, who was proprietor of the York Theatre up to 1741,

I cannot but take notice that it hath been insinuated very much to my prejudice, That neither myself nor my wife, have been sufficiently thankful for the favours which have been done us in coming to our benefits.'[32]

He then makes his excuses and professions of servility.

[29] Sybil Rosenfeld, *The Theatrical Notebooks of T. H. Wilson Manly* in *Theatre Notebook*, Vol. VII, No. 1 (1952).
[30] Minute Books of the Theatre Royal, Norwich, Vol. 1.
[31] Robert King, *op. cit.*, p. 49.
[32] Tate Wilkinson, *The Wandering Patentee*, II, 205.

LIST OF AUTHORITIES
Books Quoted In The Notes

Life of Mrs Abington, London, 1888.
John Adolphus, *Memoirs of John Bannister, Comedian,* London, 1939.
James Agate, *Those Were the Nights,* London, n.d.
James R. Anderson, *An Actor's Life,* Newcastle, 1902.
A. Aspinall, *Mrs Jordan and her Family,* London, 1951.

Leslie Bailey, *The Gilbert and Sullivan Book,* London, 1952.
Peter Baxter, *The Drama in Perth,* Perth, 1907.
Recollections of Paul Bedford, London, 1867.
Max Beerbohm and others, *Herbert Beerbohm Tree,* London, n.d.
Life of George Anne Bellamy, London, ed. 1785.
Fred Belton, *Random Recollections of an Old Actor,* London, 1880.
Miss Benger, *Memoirs of Mr John Tobin,* London, 1820.
John Bernard, *Retrospections of the Stage,* London, 1930.
Biographical Memoir of William West Betty, London, 1805.
Walter Beyham, *The Glasgow Stage,* Glasgow, 1892.
Memoirs of Mrs Billington, London, 1792.
James Boaden, *Life of Mrs Jordan,* London, 1831.
James Boaden, *Life of Mrs Siddons,* London, ed. 1827.
Alfred Bunn, *The Stage, both Before and Behind the Curtain,* London, 1840.

Mrs Charles Calvert, *Sixty-eight Years on the Stage,* London, 1911.
A Narrative of the Life of Mrs Charlotte Charke, London, ed. 1929.
Harold Child, 'Stage History of Hamlet', in New Cambridge Shakespeare ed. *Hamlet,* Cambridge, 1934.
Colley Cibber, *Apology for the Life of Mr Colley Cibber, Comedian,* London, ed. 1756.
John Cole, *Life and Times of Charles Kean,* London, 1859.
John Coleman, *Fifty Years of an Actor's Life,* London, 1904.
William Cotton, *The Story of the Drama in Exeter,* Exeter, 1887.
Joe Cowell, *Thirty Years Passed Among the Players,* London and New York, 1844.
Memoirs of Richard Cumberland, London, 1807.
J. E. Cunningham, *Theatre Royal, Birmingham,* Oxford, 1950.

Thomas Davies, *Memoirs of the Life of David Garrick,* London, 1780.
The Professional Life of Mr Dibdin, Dublin, 1791.

Thomas Dibdin, *Reminiscences,* London, 1827.
Letters between Mr West Digges and Mrs Sarah Ward, 1752-1759, Edinburgh, 1833.

Walter Donaldson, *Recollections of an Actor,* London, 1865.
J. Doran, *Their Majesties' Servants,* London, ed. 1897.
William Dunlop, *Memoirs of G. F. Cooke,* London and New York, 1813.
Robert Dyer, *Nine Years of an Actor's Life,* London and Plymouth, 1833.

S. M. Ellis, *Life of Michael Kelly,* London, 1930.
E. C. Everard, *Memoirs of an Unfortunate Son of Thespis,* Edinburgh, 1818.

Edward Fitzball, *Thirty-Five Years of a Dramatic Author's Life,* London, 1859.
Percy Fitzgerald, *Life of Mrs Clive,* London, 1888.
Percy Fitzgerald, *Life of David Garrick,* London, 1868.
Francis Fleetwood, *Conquest,* London, 1953.
Basil Francis, *Fanny Kelly of Drury Lane,* London, 1950.
John Fyvie, *Comedy Queens of the Georgian Era,* London, 1906.

The Private Correspondence of David Garrick, ed. Boaden, London, 1831.
John Genest, *Some Account of the English Stage. From the Restoration in 1660 to 1830,* Bath, 1832.
Charles Gildon, *Life of Thomas Betterton,* London, 1710.
Walter Goodmer, *The Keeleys, On the Stage and At Home,* London, 1895.

Bosworth Harcourt, *The Theatre Royal, Norwich,* Norwich, 1903.
H. N. Hildebrand, *Edmund Kean,* New York, 1933.
Robert Hitchcock, *An Historical View of the Irish Stage from the earliest period down to the close of the season 1788,* Dublin, 1788.
Charles B. Hogan, *Shakespeare in the Theatre, 1701-1800 (London 1701-1750),* London, 1952.
Mrs Holbrook, *Memoirs of an Actress,* Manchester, 1807.

John Jackson, *History of the Scottish Stage,* Edinburgh, 1793.
Jerome K. Jerome, *On the Stage, and Off,* London, n.d.

Robert King, *The Theatres of North Shields,* Gateshead, 1948.

W. J. Lawrence, *Life of Gustavus Vaughan Brooke*, Belfast, 1892.
W. J. Lawrence, *Old Theatre Days and Ways*, London, 1935.

Henry Lee, *Memoirs of a Manager*, Taunton, 1930.
E. L. Levy, Birmingham, *Theatrical Reminiscences*, Birmingham, n.d.
Charles Lee Lewis, *Memoirs*, London, 1805.
Liverpool Theatrical Investigator, Liverpool, 1821.
Robert W. Lowe, *Life of Thomas Betterton*, London, 1891.
Janet Camden Lucey, *Lovely Peggy*, London, 1952.

Malcolm Mackintosh, *Stage Reminiscences*, Glasgow, 1866.
Macready's Diaries ed. Toynbee, London, 1912.
W. C. Macready, *Reminiscences*, ed. Pollock, London, 1875.
Mrs Mathews, *Memoirs of Charles Mathews, Comedian*, London, 1838.
J. Fitzgerald Molloy, *The Romance of the Irish Stage*, London, 1897.
Memoirs of J. S. Munden, by His Son, London, 1846.

Allardyce Nicoll, *XVIIIth Century Drama 1700-1750*, Cambridge, 1925.
Allardyce Nicoll, *Restoration Drama 1660-1700*, Cambridge, 2nd ed. 1928.
Allardyce Nicoll, *Late XVIIIth Century Drama 1750-1800*, Cambridge, 2nd ed. 1952.

Recollections of the Life of John O'Keeffe, London, 1926.
Harold Oswald, *The Theatres Royal in Newcastle upon Tyne*, Newcastle, 1936.
"Peter Paterson", *Glimpses of Real Life, as seen in the Theatrical World and in Bohemia*, Edinburgh, 1864.
Richard Brinsley Peake, *Memoirs of the Colman Family*, London, 1841.
Charles E. Pearce, *Madame Vestris and Her Times*, London, n.d.
T. Edgar Pemberton, *Memoir of E. A. Sothern*, London, 4th ed. 1890.
S. Penley, *The Bath Stage*, London, 1892.
Samuel Pepys, *Diary*, 1877.
J. R. Planché, *Recollections and Reflections*, London, 1872.
Giles Playfair, *Kean*, London, 1939.
H. C. Porter, *History of the Theatres of Brighton from 1774 to 1886*, Brighton, 1886.
Cecil Price, *The English Theatre in Wales*, Cardiff, 1948.

George Raymond, *Life and Enterprises of Robert William Elliston*, London, 1857.

Thomas Leman Rede, *The Road to the Stage*, London, 1827.

E. Reid and H. Compton, *The Dramatic Peerage 1892*, London, 1892.

Elizabeth Robins, *Both Sides of the Curtain*, London, 1940.

Sybil Rosenfeld, *Actors in Bristol 1741-8,* T.L.S. August 29, 1936.

Sybil Rosenfeld, *The Theatrical Notebooks of T. H. Wilson Manley*, in Theatre Notebook, VII, No. 1, 1952.

S. W. Ryley, *The Itinerant*, London, 1817.

Clement Scott and Cecil Howard, *Edward Leman Blanchard*, London, 1891.

Thomas Snagg, *Recollections of Occurrences*, London, 1951.

Emily Soldene, *My Theatrical and Musical Recollections*, London, 1897.

Edward Stirling, *Old Drury Lane*, London, 1881.

Life of Mrs Sumbel, Late Wells, London, 1811.

Lester Wallack, *Memoirs of Fifty Years*, London, 1889.

G. T. Watts, *Theatrical Bristol*, Bristol, 1915.

Amatory Biography of Mrs Waylett, London, n.d.

Tate Wilkinson, *Memoirs of His Own Life*, Dublin, 1791.

Tate Wilkinson, *The Wandering Patentee*, York, 1795.

John Williams ("Anthony Pasquin"), *The Eccentricities of John Edwin*, London, 1791.

Julian C. Young, *Memoir of Charles Mayne Young*, London, 1871.

M. J. Young, *Memoirs of Mrs Crouch*, London, 1806.

INDEXES

PLAYS

PLAYERS

CHARACTERS IN PLAYS

GENERAL